RAISING THE BAR

Raising the Bar

Ruth Bader Ginsburg
and the ACLU Women's
Rights Project

Amy Leigh Campbell

To order additional copies of this book, contact:
Xlibris Corporation
1-888-795-4274
www.Xlibris.com
Orders@Xlibris.com
20120

Contents

For Kaki and Bob
My Favorite People in the World
Also Known as Mom and Dad

ACKNOWLEDGEMENTS

I extend my love and gratitude to those who supported me throughout this process. I am abundantly grateful to my mother and father, whose blessed marriage created a home where my creativity and curiosity were encouraged to bloom from a very young age. While writing this book I came across a journal my mother had given me for my eighth birthday. Inside, she wrote "may you fill this with your many wonderful imaginations." I readily adopted her concept that writing was a pleasure and a privilege. That lesson is one I think all children should be given.

In addition to my family, without whom I would not have an insatiable appetite for learning, several friends and mentors deserve mention. Cordel Faulk, Becca Jackson, Steve Bragaw, Ned Moomaw, and Mark Harvey are blessings and I am in their debt. I am also grateful for the group of women outside my mother and grandmothers who adopted me and continue to help me navigate my professional life. Barbara Perry and Sharon Davie, in particular, have greatly influenced my life. My colleagues at NARAL Pro-Choice America have also been supportive of my efforts to publish my work. Special thanks also go to the women of the *Texas Journal of Women and the Law* who published this work in its first incarnation.

I applaud the staff members of the Manuscripts Division of the Library of Congress who are an impressive group, especially Janice Ruth, who guided me through the early days of research.

She was instrumental in helping me gain access to materials in the private collections of Justices Brennan and Douglas, which aided my research enormously. I am also pleased to have been in contact with Lenora Lapidus, who is the current Director of the ACLU Women's Rights Project. She was gracious enough to craft the foreword for this book and I look forward to conducting more research into the WRP with her assistance.

This book began as my Master's thesis, and when completed, I nervously sent Justice Ginsburg a copy. I wasn't sure what to expect, but hoped perhaps she would be flattered and might send a note of acknowledgement. Two weeks later, I received the manuscript I originally sent her, and to my complete surprise and sheer delight, it was full of comments in the margins. There were a few points on which I was mistaken, but there were also those wonderful ones where I was exactly right. Joy!

I extend my heartfelt appreciation to Justice Ginsburg, whose courage is an inspiration to my generation. The opportunity to pursue this line of research was an unparalleled privilege in my life.

FOREWORD

It is my pleasure to introduce this tribute to Ruth Bader Ginsburg who as a lawyer, professor, women's rights advocate, and now Associate Justice of the United States Supreme Court, transformed constitutional jurisprudence to guarantee women's equality under the law. The start of this transformation took place in the 1970s, during the decade that Ginsburg founded and served as director of the Women's Rights Project (WRP) of the American Civil Liberties Union (ACLU). It was during that decade, and based in large part on the arguments put forward by Ginsburg, that the Supreme Court for the first time held that the United States Constitution prohibits discrimination against women.

The pioneering cases litigated by Ginsburg in the 1970s set the standard for the work of the WRP in the three decades that have followed. Much progress has been made in the last 30 years. Yet, a great deal of work remains to be done. The discrimination the WRP encounters and fights today is less blatant, more subtle, and therefore more difficult to uncover and address. Moreover, although today's laws require equal treatment of men and women, not all women benefit from these laws, either because they are unaware of them or lack the resources to enforce them. A primary goal of the WRP today, therefore, is to ensure that all women—regardless of race, ethnicity, or economic status—can attain true equality.

As director of the ACLU Women's Rights Project, then-professor Ruth Bader Ginsburg set her sights high: to guarantee equal treatment for women as a constitutionally protected right. She laid the groundwork for this constitutional protection as a litigator in the 1970s landmark Supreme Court cases including, *Reed v. Reed, Frontiero v. Richardson, Weinberger v. Weisenfeld,* and *Craig v. Boren.* She further developed the theories for women's equal rights as a professor at Rutgers Law School and Columbia Law School. Then, in 1996, as Associate Justice of the Supreme Court, Ginsburg placed the capstone on this pursuit for constitutional equality with her decision in *United States v. Virginia,* in which the Court struck down the all-male admissions policy at the state-sponsored military academy known as VMI. With this decision, the Court for the first time applied a heightened standard of review requiring the government to demonstrate an "exceedingly persuasive justification" for any law or action that differentiates on the basis of gender. The ACLU Women's Rights Project, with Ginsburg at the helm and after her departure, was involved throughout this long struggle, developing the legal theories, writing the briefs, and arguing the cases before the Supreme Court.

In some ways, the battles fought in the 1970s are still being waged today. For example, in one of the WRP's early cases, *Weinberger v. Weisenfeld,* then-Professor Ginsburg successfully argued that a provision of the Social Security Act providing for gender-based distinctions in the award of social security benefits—whereby benefits to care for a child were provided to widows with minor children but not to widowers—was unconstitutional. In arguing this case on behalf of Stephen Weisenfeld, whose wife had died in childbirth, Professor Ginsburg established not only that gender discrimination harms men as well women, but also that true equality will only prevail when men are seen as equal partners in parenting and family obligations and women are seen as equal colleagues in the workforce. This struggle to create an environment that supports men and women in their efforts to balance work and family obligations continues today. In *Knussman v. State of Maryland*, for example, the WRP and the ACLU of Maryland represent Kevin Knussman, a Maryland state trooper who was denied family medical leave upon the birth of his daughter, although the state police allow women to take leave upon the birth of a child. In this case, notwithstanding the mandate of the Family Medical Leave Act (FMLA), which requires employers to provide leave to *any* employee to care for a newborn or newly adopted child (as well as to care for a seriously ill family member or for oneself when suffering a serious illness), the state applied sex-role stereotypes to decide that mothers, but not fathers, were entitled to take leave to care for an infant. That family leave must be equally available for men and women to overcome a history of sex-role stereotyping was recently reaffirmed by the Supreme Court, with Justice Ginsburg in the majority, in *Nevada Department of Human Resources v. Hibbs*, in which the Court held that a government employee could sue his employer for violations of the FMLA.

While some of the struggles we fight today are the same as those we fought in the 1970s, in other cases our litigation has shifted from challenging formal inequality—laws or policies that discriminate on their face—to addressing structural exclusion—subtle and overt forms of gender disadvantage and prejudice perpetuated through market, political and social mechanisms. Thus, a major goal of the WRP today is to ensure that *all* women benefit from the legal victories we have achieved—particularly low-income women and women of color—and to make equal rights a reality for women (and girls) in every stratum of society. Thus, for example, we address employment discrimination faced by low-income immigrant women and women in non-traditional employment. In addition, because women, especially single mothers, are at disproportionate risk of poverty as a result of their care-giving responsibilities and the continuing obstacles facing women seeking high-wage employment, poverty is an important issue for the WRP. Further, because women and children are the vast majority of recipients of Temporary Assistance for Needy Families (TANF), and thus are the ones primarily affected by the welfare program's punitive policies, discriminatory practices, and due process failures, welfare is an important women's rights issue and is a high priority for the WRP. As a result, we are currently challenging punitive welfare "reform" measures, such as child exclusion policies that deny welfare benefits to any child born into a family already receiving aid. These child exclusion laws, or "family caps," unfairly punish an innocent child for the conduct of his or her parent and infringe on women's right to decide whether and when to bear a child. In addition, we are investigating racial disparities and gender steering in welfare programs.

In all of our efforts, we work closely with ACLU affiliate offices around the country, just as Ginsburg did during her years as director of the Women's Rights Project. The ACLU's unique structure, then and now, has enabled the WRP to be influential in bringing about broad-based, nationwide systemic change. Because the ACLU has staffed affiliate offices and chapters in every state in the country, we are aware of problems facing women, on the ground, in every region of the United States. Further, we are able to develop strategies to confront the problems and then implement those strategies locally throughout the country. Indeed, shortly after I became director of the WRP in 2001, Justice Ginsburg graciously invited me to a private meeting in her chambers at the Supreme Court. When I asked her what she thought were the most important women's rights issues today, she humbly responded, "You would know better than I, based on the types of complaints that are brought to the affiliates." I take to heart Justice Ginsburg's implied advice, that we must develop our priorities by listening to the concerns of women from across the country. As we move forward, I hope to heed the import of Justice Ginsburg's words and work to harness the resources of the ACLU's vast network even more in an attempt to reveal and redress the problems facing "invisible" women-low-income women, women of color, immigrant women, battered women, and women in prison. Finally, in addition to expanding legal rights to reach all women, the WRP also seeks to expand the bases from which these rights derive. For example, we are working to develop ways to use international human rights norms in domestic litigation, recognizing, as Justice Ginsburg has urged, that the United States is part of an international community and that we can gain a great deal by looking beyond our own borders as we seek to enforce equal rights for all people.

Justice Ginsburg has been an inspiration to those of us working to ensure women's equality. She is both a role model and a mentor. Following in her footsteps as director of the WRP is a formidable challenge. Yet, I carry this mantle with eagerness and pride. I am honored to have the opportunity to lead the ACLU's fight for women's rights—through our work at the WRP, our collaboration with ACLU affiliates across the country, and our support of the ACLU's National Legislative Office. This thorough and cogent book is a tribute to Ginsburg's brilliant litigation strategies and legal successes as well as the historic role played by the ACLU as one of the earliest organizers for women's rights. Since its founding in 1920, the ACLU has fought for women's equal participation in society. I am proud of our history and I look forward to continuing this great legacy as the WRP fights to secure full equality for all women in the 21st Century.

Lenora Lapidus
Director, ACLU Women's Rights Project

INTRODUCTION

This book defines the contribution of Ruth Bader Ginsburg to American constitutional law through her efforts as professor, lawyer, and women's rights advocate. The research focuses primarily on the years 1971 to 1980, during which time Ginsburg founded and was General Counsel to the American Civil Liberties Union Women's Rights Project. Although her activities covered a broad range during those years, the concentration is on the litigation strategies she developed and employed in her roles as amicus curiae (hereinafter amicus), co-counsel, and lead counsel before the United States Supreme Court. From 1971 to 1980, Ginsburg participated in thirty-four cases. The majority of these are explored herein, with landmark cases examined in greater detail. The construction of the briefs in early cases is explored in particular detail as these arguments illustrate the unique intellectual analysis Ginsburg incorporated into her successful litigation strategy. Her method of taking extra-legal factors into account in her legal arguments is a hallmark of her strategy. In addition, her keen instinct, combined with meticulous research and preparation, allowed her to target the Justices psychologically.

The primary sources of information were the private papers of now Justice Ginsburg. The collection was donated in September 1998 and is housed in the Manuscripts Division of the Library of Congress. It spans the years 1946 to 1992, with the bulk concentrated in the period 1972 to 1980. The majority of the collection consists of papers documenting Ginsburg's work as an advocate for women's rights, particularly through her speeches, writings, and other documentation of her efforts as general counsel to the Women's Rights Project.

The papers comprise three categories: the American Civil Liberties Union file, the Speeches and Writings file, and the Miscellany file. The ACLU file, covering 1967 to 1980, comprises nearly half the collection. The files include correspondence and memoranda, primarily between Ginsburg and clients, lawyers, clerks, and ACLU colleagues, as well as an array of legal papers such as opinions, orders, briefs, and motions. The Speeches and Writings file, spanning 1967 to 1980, consists chiefly of Ginsburg's speeches and articles. The speeches fall into two main categories. Those in the first set were delivered at conferences and meetings of women's rights groups and provide an interesting look at how Ginsburg viewed the progress of her litigation strategy. The speeches in the second set document Ginsburg's effort as a proponent for the passage of the Equal Rights Amendment (ERA) and include various statements before numerous state legislatures during the ratification period. The Miscellany file, covering 1946 to 1992, includes a truly miscellaneous collection of notes on ERA advocacy strategy, drafts of academic papers, and personal correspondence.

Secondary sources included books and articles about judicial decision-making and strategic interaction on the Supreme Court. This information was valuable in determining what was publicly known about the Justices' preferences when cases arrived at the Supreme Court. This created an avenue for speculation about the factors Ginsburg considered in formulating her litigation strategy. For example, in *The Choices Justices Make*,[1] Lee Epstein and Jack Knight detail Justice Brennan's strategic actions in writing the opinion for the Court in *Frontiero v. Richardson*.[2] Memoranda and correspondence between Ginsburg and fellow counsel on cases suggest that she tailored her oral arguments to specific Justices. In several cases, she was in direct contact with Supreme Court clerks and exchanged information with such individuals about the inner workings of the Court. This is not to suggest that Ginsburg was privy to confidential information or engaged in improper activity—rather that she benefited from a collegial relationship with Court clerks in crafting her strategy. Finally, in an effort to understand such an accomplished, yet very private, woman, two former clerks, Elizabeth Magill and Michael Klarman, were interviewed for my original law review article. They provided valuable anecdotal information about the human side of a unique individual.

The research was also aided by an extensive paper trail, including published pieces in journals and law reviews, left by Ginsburg that details the evolution of her theories concerning the relationship between litigation against sex-based discrimination and the Fourteenth Amendment.[3] She wrote several pieces during her years with the ACLU and continued to publish after her appointment to the federal bench. Her work published in the late 1970s largely reflects her commitment to and continued advocacy for a stricter level of review in judging gender discrimination cases.

A defining characteristic of Ginsburg in this period was her in-depth understanding of the limitations of the judicial branch. Not to be confused with complacency, this understanding of the Supreme Court's role did not dissuade her from suggesting in speeches and articles that applying the Fourteenth Amendment[4] only to racial discrimination might deter dynamic judicial interpretation in adjudicating cases of sex discrimination. There is a marked difference in her approach after the failure of the states to ratify the ERA. Before the period for ratification had expired, Ginsburg argued for the ERA as the necessary tool for the Court to overcome the purported lack of a historical basis for sexual equality in the law, which was keeping the Court from painting broader strokes against sex discrimination. After she left the ACLU,

Ginsburg's published work reflected on the social and legal changes she helped bring about in the 1970s.

The book is organized into five chapters. Chapters One and Two provide background information about both Ginsburg and the Women's Rights Project. Chapters Three through Five are organized to reflect Ginsburg's categorization of the three stages of her strategy—1971 began "forward movement," 1974 signaled "line holding and retrenchment," and 1975 put the strategy "back on track."[5] These chapter titles use the phrases that she herself coined. Words and phrases that she used to describe particular cases are used to title subheadings whenever appropriate.

The purpose of this book is not to provide further evidence for the effect of a calculated litigation strategy since the legal and academic communities are in agreement as to its impact. Although the analysis of her efforts as general counsel for the Women's Rights Project does provide a deeper understanding of Ginsburg's lasting contribution, the goal of this book is to pinpoint Ginsburg's role in the *progression* of such a complicated, multi-layered strategy from *theory* to *implementation*. Scholars and law students have undertaken similar analyses to some degree in the past, but the missing ingredient has long been Ginsburg's own perspective, now made available by the collection of materials that Justice Ginsburg has graciously donated.

CHAPTER I
"A WOMAN, A MOTHER, AND A JEW"[6]

Joan Ruth Bader was born to Nathan and Celia Bader on March 15, 1933, in Brooklyn, New York. Despite the traditional role assigned girls in the Bader's ethnic neighborhood, Ruth's mother taught her to be independent and saved money for her college tuition. Her academic prowess became apparent early; she graduated first in her class from New York's P.S. 238, and sixth from James Madison High School. She continued her studies as a scholarship student at Cornell University where she was named Phi Beta Kappa and again graduated first in her class.[7]

It was during her freshman year that she met Martin Ginsburg, whom she married in 1954, following her graduation and his first year at Harvard Law School. Ruth Ginsburg also enrolled at Harvard for legal education in a class of only nine women, and over 500 men. During her two years there, she earned a spot on the *Harvard Law Review*, despite the responsibility of mothering her daughter, Jane, and at times performing the work of two law students when Martin fell ill with testicular cancer. With amazing fortitude, she performed at the top of her own class while gathering notes from her husband's classmates and typing his third year paper for him. Upon Martin's recovery and subsequent graduation, he accepted an offer with a firm in New York, where the family

moved and Ruth Ginsburg enrolled in Columbia University
Law School for her final year. She was named to the *Columbia
Law Review* and graduated first in her class.

At both institutions, Ginsburg entered an environment
that she found to be unfriendly to women. At a Harvard dinner,
she was asked how she could justify taking a place that should
rightfully be occupied by a man. This ritual was an annual
one for Dean Erwin Griswold, who sought to be armed with
answers for colleagues who still questioned the wisdom of
admitting women to the Harvard Law School. Ginsburg has
characterized his comments as an attempt at humor, but
disquieting to the women nonetheless. She talked about the
experience, confessing, "[i]n those days I smoked, . . . and when
it came my turn [to answer] the ashtray I was sharing with . . .
Herbert Wechsler slid . . . onto the floor . . . . All I could think
of to say was that my husband was in the second year class and
it was important for a wife to understand her husband's work."[8]

Despite her stellar credentials, Ginsburg entered the work
force in an era where few federal judges, and certainly no
Supreme Court Justices, were willing to hire female clerks.
She was recommended to Justice Felix Frankfurter by Professor
Gerald Gunther and Professor—later Dean—Albert Sacks,
but Frankfurter declined her services, replying that he was
unwilling to break the tradition of hiring only male clerks,[9]
although he was the first Supreme Court Justice to hire an
African-American clerk. Professor Gunther succeeded in
placing Ginsburg with a Columbia graduate, Judge Edmund
L. Palmieri of the United States District Court for the Southern
District of New York. Palmieri agreed after a great deal of
persuasion from Gunther, and after receiving a male student's
assurance that he would leave his law firm to take Ginsburg's
place if she did not work out.[10] Soon after her placement,
Ginsburg earned her stripes with Palmieri. As he was preparing
to rule on a motion, she brought to his attention a pending
Supreme Court case that both lawyers had neglected to
mention. The case proved dispositive.[11] Palmieri was so

impressed with the woman on whom he had taken a chance, he hired another female clerk the following year.[12]

Indeed, several firms who offered Ginsburg positions subsequent to her clerkship had noticed her performance under Palmieri's tutelage. She decided instead to accept a position on the Columbia Project on International Civil Procedure, headed by Columbia professor Hans Smit. She co-authored a book on Swedish Civil Procedure, for which she was awarded an honorary doctorate by the University of Lund.[13] Concurrent to her work with the Columbia Project on International Civil Procedure, Ginsburg accepted a position at Rutgers where she served from 1963 to 1972.[14] At Rutgers she consulted on several sex discrimination cases that were referred to her by the American Civil Liberties Union (ACLU) and developed a passion for women's rights. She was inspired and encouraged by her students, as well as the women referred to her, to take an active part in the growing women's movement.[15] One of those women was Sally Reed, who would become the litigant in the first case in which Ginsburg participated with ACLU Director Mel Wulf.[16]

In her decade of service under the banner of the ACLU Women's Rights Project, Ginsburg took part in 34 cases at the Supreme Court level, arguing six as lead or co-counsel, and winning five.[17] The ultimate goal of the litigation strategy she spearheaded was to elevate gender-based classifications to the level of a suspect category for review purposes. Although that goal was never realized, she was successful in convincing the Court to adopt an intermediate tier of review, which remains the standard.[18] From 1976, when this test was first announced, until 1996 when the Virginia Military Institute (VMI) case was written[19] by now Justice Ginsburg, "heightened scrutiny" was the standard in determining whether the equal protection of the laws had been denied a defendant challenging sex discrimination. In the VMI case, Justice Ginsburg wrote that states must present an "exceedingly persuasive justification" to deny women access to a state-funded institution.[20] Although the opinion does not technically raise the level of scrutiny afforded gender-based classifications, Justice Scalia noted that the language made review "strict in theory and fatal in fact."[21] Many constitutional law scholars and court watchers agreed with Justice Scalia, giving credibility to the argument that Ginsburg may have achieved, or certainly will achieve, her goal in the long run.

CHAPTER II
GENESIS OF THE ACLU
WOMEN'S RIGHTS PROJECT

In 1987, then United States Circuit Court Judge Ruth Bader Ginsburg noted that, except for the Nineteenth Amendment, "the Constitution remained an empty cupboard for sex equality claims."[22] One of the earliest organizers for women's rights was the American Civil Liberties Union. Nadine Strossen, current President of the ACLU, has written that the public at large is most familiar with the ACLU in the area of classic civil and political liberties, such as free speech and the rights of the criminally accused.[23] Yet the ACLU has also been instrumental in the advancement of the rights of traditionally disempowered groups, including religious and racial minorities, women, and homosexuals.[24] Since its inception in 1920, the American Civil Liberties Union has recognized that the rights of women as a group in American society are inextricably linked with the broader agenda of advancing civil liberties.[25] Although the founding of the ACLU preceded the adoption of the Nineteenth Amendment by several months, women occupied positions of leadership in the organization from the very beginning.[26]

Among the founding mothers of the ACLU were Jane Addams (1869-1935) and Emily Greene Balch (1867-1961), both of whom were named Nobel Peace Laureates in recognition of their work for international peace and freedom.[27]

Women's contributions in the conception and development of the ACLU were fundamental because the ACLU was born out of the interests of women who were concerned with the problems of war and peace.

Wasting no time, the ACLU began the long struggle for the advancement of women's rights as early as 1922, defending the distribution of a sex education pamphlet that had been declared by the U.S. Postal Service to be "obscene."[28] Fifteen years later, it fought on behalf of female schoolteachers in Connecticut who sought to return to their jobs following their children's birth,[29] foreshadowing a cause that Ruth Bader Ginsburg would eventually champion in the late 1960s. Throughout the 1940s and 1950s, the ACLU established committees to advocate the advancement of women's rights as a priority in their agenda. The Committee on Women's Rights, established in 1945, eventually merged with the Race Relations Committee to form the Equality Committee in 1956.[30]

The 1960s ushered in a new wave of feminist activism. Throughout the United States, women's sense of self was awakened by Betty Friedan's book *The Feminine Mystique*,[31] and feminists were becoming furious with Phyllis Schlafly and her Eagle Forum.[32] Change was inevitable. Originally opposed to the Equal Rights Amendment on the grounds that it would nullify protective labor legislation for women workers, the ACLU eventually reversed its position in response to the arguments of women scholars and activists, among them Ruth Bader Ginsburg, who criticized the motives behind such classifications.[33] Discrimination based on sex was being exposed as contradicting its labels "benign" and "harmless," even "protective."[34] During this time, the ACLU took an early stand against laws criminalizing abortion and homosexual relationships based on the work of pioneers Dorothy Kenyon, Pauli Murray, and Harriet Pilpel.[35] In 1966, Dorothy Kenyon had won an important victory for women's rights in the ACLU's successful challenge to an Alabama statute exempting women from juries.[36] That case tempered the blow to women's full equality in *Hoyt v. Florida*,[37] five years earlier, and gave legal recognition to the motives behind legislation that purported to protect women and preserve the sanctity of the home.[38]

The 1970s brought the issue of women's full participation as members of society to the forefront of the national consciousness. The ACLU's Board of Directors declared women's rights to be their top legal and legislative priority in December 1971, following the victory in *Reed v. Reed*.[39] The Board hired Professor Ruth Bader Ginsburg to found and direct the Women's Rights Project (WRP) in the spring of 1972 in recognition of her successful collaboration with ACLU attorney Mel Wulf. Sex discrimination complaints had been filed in the New Jersey ACLU since the late 1960s. They were referred to Ginsburg because, in her words, "sex discrimination cases were regarded as a woman's job."[40] She accepted the responsibility in part because her meetings with members of the Kentucky and Illinois ACLU affiliates left her with the impression that many ACLU lawyers were not enthusiastic about taking on women's rights cases. She was also concerned that few women served on the ACLU's own governing board.[41]

From the outset, the project was a nationwide effort with ACLU affiliates in every state working in coordination with Ginsburg and Brenda Feigen Fasteau.[42] Ginsburg came to work with the ACLU because she felt that the organization was the appropriate vehicle for her activism in two important ways: the national structure would allow the WRP to identify cases across the country, and the shared philosophy between Ginsburg and the ACLU concerning the integral link between civil rights and civil liberties.[43] Ginsburg has said that she wanted gender-based discrimination "to be part of a general human rights agenda. Civil liberties are an essential part of the overall human rights concern—the equality of all people and the ability to be free."[44] Indeed, the 1972 prospectus for the WRP took a page from the civil rights agenda:

The experience of trying to root out racial discrimination in the United States has demonstrated that even when the arsenal of legislative and judicial remedies is well stocked, social and cultural institutions shaped by centuries of law sanctioned bias do not crumble under the weight of legal pronouncements proscribing discrimination.[45]

The WRP was based on the concept that sexual equality would be most effectively realized by systematic litigation in the courts that redressed discrimination against women. Within the ACLU, the WRP had the resources, commitment, and structure to lead the fight on behalf of women's rights. In 1972, women were beginning to develop some protection of their equal rights. Federal measures offering relief from discriminatory employment practices were passing Congress,[46] and Presidents had signed executive orders to eliminate discrimination against women in federal positions.[47]

While many observers hailed the rapid progress of women in the workforce, Ginsburg knew that although federal measures, like Title IX,[48] were important, their coverage was limited. Her reluctance to rely on these measures for continued progress was a crucial decision for the WRP; between 1972 and 1991, not a single offending school lost a dollar of federal funds under Title IX.[49] The measures in place when the WRP came into existence were directed solely at employment—an area where many offending employers were not subject to the legislation. In addition, areas outside the workplace were not affected by governmental measures. Ginsburg created the WRP to provide focus and direction to litigation exposing and seeking to eradicate the discrimination in those uncharted waters.

Ginsburg and Fasteau identified six core areas in which the WRP would work to effect change. These included employment issues, discriminatory governmental aid to private institutions, reproductive control, admissions policies in educational institutions, government training programs, and discrimination in credit.[50] Their strategy in these areas incorporated direct and indirect assistance by counsel, publication of materials informing women of their rights, work with legislatures in revising discriminatory laws, and conferences and training programs for attorneys active in litigating sex discrimination issues.[51]

Ginsburg believed that, until 1971, the Supreme Court had been faithful to the original understanding of the Constitution and the Fourteenth Amendment. Neither the Founding Fathers nor the Reconstruction Congress had questioned two fundamental assumptions.[52] The first, that a woman's place in the world was controlled by men and was divinely ordained, was an assumption reflected in Justice Bradley's concurring opinion in *Bradwell v. Illinois*.[53] Myra Bradwell had been denied admission to the bar solely on the basis of her gender, the Court holding that the right to practice law was not one of the privileges of citizenship. The Court did not consider the Due Process and Equal Protection Clauses, in light of the *Slaughter-House Cases*[54] decided the year before, where the Court explicitly stated that the Equal Protection provision was designed solely to check racial discrimination.[55] Ginsburg noted that the Court's refusal to ascribe to the Fourteenth Amendment's Privileges and Immunities clause was predictable without regard to any sexist assumptions, because the Court in the *Slaughter-House Cases* had ruled out any independent scope for application of that clause.[56]

The second assumption was that the law's different treatment of a woman operated benignly in her favor. Ginsburg identified three cases based on that assumption.

Muller v. Oregon upheld a maximum work hours restriction for women because of the "inherent differences between the two sexes" and the "different functions in life, which [men and women] perform."[57] Although dismayed by the blatant male supremacy expressed in the opinion, Ginsburg noted, "short of overruling *Lochner* . . . what alternative did the *Muller* Court have?"[58] She was less willing to find defensible grounds for the 1948 decision in *Goesaert v. Cleary*, where the Court refused to allow women to be employed as bartenders, effectively drawing "a sharp line between the sexes"[59] that was still in place two decades later. The third case, *Hoyt v. Florida*,[60] was the worst offender in this trilogy, limiting the service of women on juries to volunteers. The Court held that a woman should not be required to serve because she "is still regarded as the center of home and family life."[61] In Ginsburg's view, a declaration by the Court that women had the right, but not the responsibility, to serve as jurors, was as detrimental as the denial of the right itself. Ginsburg declared two priorities for the WRP: to challenge specific gender-based discrimination under the law and to eliminate discrimination based on pregnancy. With regard to the first priority, Ginsburg placed the four aforementioned decisions on the short list for the WRP to persuade the Supreme Court to overturn.[62]

CHAPTER III
FORWARD MOVEMENT

THE GRANDMOTHER BRIEF

When Ginsburg entered the legal and political arena to fight for gender equality, she did so with a keen awareness of the torch that an earlier generation of activists had passed to her.[63] Women like Dorothy Kenyon and Pauli Murray paved the way for Ginsburg and her colleagues. Ginsburg once remarked that "[i]t was much easier for us to do what we did . . . there were a lot of things that were very hard for [that generation]."[64] Co-authoring the *Reed* brief with ACLU Director Mel Wulf,[65] she placed the names of Kenyon and Murray on the title page as a symbolic gesture of the "intellectual debt which contemporary feminist legal argument owed [them]."[66] It was, after all, Murray's *Jane Crow and the Law*,[67] written with Mary Eastwood, that Ginsburg used to develop materials for one of the first law school courses devoted to gender discrimination.[68]

Reed v. Reed[69] was orally argued at the Supreme Court level, not by Ginsburg, but by Sally Reed's original Idaho lawyer. Ginsburg co-authored the brief for Sally Reed with Wulf while still teaching full-time at Rutgers, and was assisted by several of her brightest students in addition to several from NYU.[70] The case involved a teenage boy from Idaho, Richard Lynn Reed, who committed suicide. His parents were long separated and had each held custody of Richard at different points in his life. Richard was placed with his mother during his "tender years," and sent to live with his father by order of the Court for his "manhood years."[71] His death followed a period of time spent in a corrections facility and a severe bout of depression. Sally Reed sought to be named the administrator of her son's estate. Days later the father applied for the same appointment. Although Sally Reed's application was first in time, Idaho appointed the father in accordance with §§15-312 and 15-314 of the Idaho code, which specified that between persons equally entitled to administer a decedent's estate, males must be preferred to females.[72] Of Sally Reed, Ginsburg has said, "[she] was not a sophisticated woman . . . . She probably did not think of herself as a feminist, but she had the strong sense that her state's law was unjust. And I sensed that she would prevail."[73]

The appellee in *Reed* urged deference to Idaho's law and the state court decision finding the preference of males over females in the probate statute constitutional.[74] Cecil Reed's terse 15 page brief criticizes Ginsburg's comparison of race discrimination to sex discrimination, asserting that no prejudice exists between men and women, whereas it can be found between races.[75] Cecil Reed's attorneys went so far as to warn the Court that finding gender to be a suspect class would, in effect, enact the Equal Rights Amendment, thereby "resulting in chaos."[76]

Ginsburg believed that *Reed* was the perfect case. It was stunningly simple, which allowed Ginsburg to dissect the motives behind the Idaho Code, and to dismantle the discrimination from every conceivable angle and arrange her argument around the larger goal of convincing the Court to declare sex a suspect class. Ginsburg argued the appellant's position on two key grounds: the state's objective would clearly fail the general test for reasonableness set forth in *F.S. Royster Guano v. Virginia*,[77] and the fact that Mrs. Reed had been denied the administration of her son's estate solely because of her sex,[78] thereby creating an "invidious" classification.[79] Such treatment, Ginsburg wrote, "constitutes arbitrary and unequal treatment proscribed by the Fourteenth Amendment of the United States Constitution."[80]

Only eight pages of the 67 page brief are devoted to arguing that the portion of the Idaho code at issue in *Reed* failed the rational relation test.[81] Under that precedential test, the statute had clearly discriminated against Sally Reed. Thus, that portion of the argument was considered the fall back position in case the Court rejected the strict scrutiny standard's application outright. Ginsburg attacked the Idaho law as arbitrary and capricious, stating that "the discrimination is so patently visible that the statute is readily assailable under the less stringent reasonable relation test."[82] Not content with a simple victory for Sally Reed, even Ginsburg's fallback position requested a change in the application of the *F.S. Royster Guano* standard mandating that all similarly situated persons be treated alike.[83] Ginsburg urged for the application of an intermediate test. She proposed that the Court reverse the presumption of rationality when the statute accorded a preference to males. Under the new system, the state would have the burden of proof concerning reasonableness, rather than the party attacking the statute.[84]

The appellee argued that the statute bore a rational relation to the supposed greater business experience of men which better qualifies them as executors of estates. Idaho also asserted the state's interest in prompt and efficient probate administration. Ginsburg agreed with the Idaho District Court judge and his opinion that a judgment about the general capabilities of men and women acting as administrators "has no basis in fact."[85] Judge Donaldson demanded the "swift condemnation of the Court."[86] The efficiency argument was also dismantled quickly by Ginsburg. Of the innumerable situations that could present themselves for hearings, the statute only "efficiently" disposed of those concerning two qualified applicants, one male and one female—a blatantly discriminatory practice. Ginsburg did not argue against the appellees' notion of the proper role of men and women as prescribed by nature, nor did she counter their argument concerning the role of the political process. Her handwritten notes in the margins of her copy of the appellees' brief, however, bear witness to her caustic wit, leading to the likely conclusion that she found the assertions too ridiculous and archaic to deserve rebuttal. Written beside the paragraph detailing reasons why nature is testimony for unequal treatment of the sexes, Ginsburg wrote "black widow spiders."[87] Where Idaho made the argument that women have the right to vote in the state, and subsequently have not used their political power to repeal the statute in question, Ginsburg declared, "Women acquiesce!"[88] When the respondents later note that as of 1971, three women had been elected to Idaho's legislature, Ginsburg wrote "so much for women acquiescing."[89]

Challenging one common stereotype of the two sexes, *Reed* questioned the specific competence of women as compared to men in business affairs.[90] To rebut the appellees' contention that men are inherently more qualified in administrating estates, Ginsburg employed statistical evidence about the increasing numbers of women in higher education and their rising levels of participation in the workforce. Ironically, the first use of that strategy before the Court resulted in discrimination *against* women, in the *Muller* case that Ginsburg placed on the short list for the WRP to work to overturn.[91] In addition to the statistical evidence, Ginsburg employed a surprisingly minimalist argument, noting that housewives often handle the family accounting and acquire managerial experience as wives and mothers.[92] Although true, this set of facts could be seen as patronizing. In a sense, she was "dumbing down" the responsibilities Sally Reed was asking to receive. A more plausible suggestion is that she was targeting the most conservative members of the Court.

Incorporating the preferences of the sitting Justices is a finely honed skill that Ginsburg possessed throughout her career as an advocate. She has written, "[t]he Supreme Court needed basic education before it was equipped to turn away from the precedents in place. . . . A teacher from outside the club . . . knows she must keep it comprehensible and digestible, not too complex or intimidating, or risk losing her audience."[93] Indeed, it is evident in *Reed* that her priority was to convince at least five of the nine justices, separately if need be, that sex should be declared a suspect class.[94] Her strategy was to include something for each of the nine Justices. Armed with more than just statistics and precedent, the standard fare of briefs, *Reed* was complete with literature, history, biology, philosophy, theology, and feminist doctrine to back her claim. The timely publication of both Gunnar Myrdal's *An American Dilemma,*[95] and Simone de Beauvoir's *The Second Sex,*[96] as well as other notable works of feminist scholarship, aided Ginsburg's mission by placing legal ideas into the mainstream. In her effort to tie together sexual and racial prejudice, she quoted extensively from such literature as confirmation of her theories by contemporary scholarship.[97] Evidence of women's inferiority was drawn from such varied sources as Henrik Ibsen's *A Doll's House*[98] and Alexis de Tocqueville's *Democracy in America.*[99] What has become known as the "grandmother brief" might rightly also be known as the "everything but the kitchen sink" brief.

Ginsburg's strategy of including extra-legal material in the brief was deemed by the appellee as wasteful, serving no useful purpose. Whether or not this extra effort contributed to the outcome in *Reed*, it did succeed in cementing Ginsburg's reputation as an advocate who left no stone unturned. Her attention to detail and abundant supply of evidence of discrimination challenged the Court to find any reason that §15-314 of the Idaho code could be found "reasonable." The bulk of the brief, and the genesis of its title as the "grandmother brief," was its devotion to the higher purpose of convincing the Court that gender, like race and alienage, encompassed a class of persons who encountered law-sanctioned obstacles without regard to the individual capabilities of members of that group. Noting the numerous federal measures passed and executive orders issued by 1971 in response to the denial of equal opportunity to women, she was politely suggesting that the Court was overdue in protecting the rights of women, as Congress and the President had both begun to recognize the unfair treatment toward women and provide remedies. In her words, declaring gender classifications inherently suspect "is the only wholly satisfactory standard for dealing with the claim in this case, and should be the starting point for assessing that claim."[100] She characterized the Court's anticipated inclination, modifying the rational basis test, as a delay tactic.[101]

Tying gender to race, she aimed squarely at the Court's pride, reminding them that the institution's refusal in *Plessy v. Ferguson*[102] to declare racial discrimination unconstitutional served to reinforce and bolster racism, "postponing for fifty-eight years the inevitable inauguration of a national commitment to abolish racial discrimination."[103] Like *Plessy*, *Reed* provided the forum to strike down discriminatory practices, and the failure to do so was the equivalent of sanctioning them. Furthermore, she reminded the Court, oppression based on race was modeled after oppression based on gender.[104] Ginsburg quoted Myrdal, who wrote, "when a legal status had to be found for the imported Negro servants in the seventeenth century, the nearest and most natural analogy was the status of women and children."[105]

The major hurdle in *Reed* was the necessity of explaining why pertinent, yet disturbing precedents should not be controlling. Of the four decisions Ginsburg would later make priorities for the WRP to work to overturn, three needed attention in *Reed*.[106] Fortunately, the Ninth Circuit had recently reconsidered *Muller v. Oregon*[107] under the microscope of the present day climate, finding several reasons why the case had no precedential value by 1971.[108] The other two, *Goesaert v. Cleary*[109] and *Hoyt v. Florida*,[110] would prove more difficult to dispatch.

Ginsburg's disdain for *Goesaert*, and for Justice Frankfurter's opinion in the case, was obvious. In the *Reed* brief, she took Frankfurter to task for allowing legislatures to overlook "sociological insight" and "shifting social standards,"[111] when the Court relied on those very tools six years later in *Brown v. Board of Education*[112] to strike down racial discrimination. She boldly admonished the Court for its decision in *Goesaert*, but credited them with steps toward redemption in *United States v. Dege*,[113] and offered *Reed* as the salve for the wounds they inflicted on themselves in a decision that scholars picked at and courts politely discarded.[114] Although Ginsburg does not mention it in the *Reed* brief, she was clearly dismayed by the difference in the majority's logic in *Goesaert* and their 1915 opinion in *Truax v. Raich*.[115] There, the Court held that "the right to work [without discrimination on the grounds of race or nationality] is of the very essence of the personal freedom and opportunity."[116] Ginsburg noted to herself that this apparently had no bearing on Frankfurter's starting point in *Goesaert*[117] that "Michigan may deny to all women opportunities for bartending."[118] Even more striking, she believed, was *Takahashi v. Fish and Game Commission*,[119] (decided the same term as *Goesaert*), which invalidated on equal protection grounds a statute denying fishing licenses to aliens ineligible for citizenship.[120] Even the dissenters in *Goesaert* did not question Frankfurter's premise. Perhaps most insulting, plaintiff's counsel in that case did not argue against the general exclusion of women, choosing instead to focus narrowly on the exception for wives and daughters of male bar owners.[121]

The facts at issue in *Hoyt v. Florida* were not directly related to the Idaho statute in *Reed*, but the Court's inclusion of discriminatory language in the decision made *Hoyt* the third in a trilogy of cases, after *Muller* and *Goesaert*, that was often used to justify second-class status for women. In 1961, the Supreme Court declined to strike down a provision of Florida law that automatically exempted women from jury duty unless they volunteered, because women were seen as the center of home and family life. Fortunately for Ginsburg, by 1971, the advancements states had made in reforming jury exemption statutes had all but mooted *Hoyt*. Moreover, a three judge federal district court in Alabama had declared total exclusion of women as jurors unconstitutional in 1966.[122] Like *Muller*, the *Hoyt* decision had established a gender classification that purported to be beneficial to women. In doing so, *Hoyt* had given lease to lower courts to contort the meaning of the "volunteers only" provision into decisions such as the 1970 *DeKosenko v. Brandt* which held that women automatically exempted from juries do not serve because they prefer "cleaning and cooking, rearing of children and television soap operas, bridge and canasta, the beauty parlor and shopping."[123]

Ginsburg could not have known at the time she argued *Reed* that in its next term, the Court would decide *Alexander v. Louisiana*,[124] which involved another "volunteers only" provision. Identical to the incompatible stance taken between *Goesaert* and *Takahashi* in 1948, the Burger Court in 1972 found that male defendants are not "denied equal protection by the exclusion . . . of women from grand jury service,"[125] yet found the exclusion of blacks from grand juries would entitle a white defendant to federal habeas corpus relief, even if he could not show that he had been harmed by such exclusion.[126] The battle to rectify that double standard would be fought in *Edwards v. Healy*,[127] two years later. Sufficient for her argument in *Reed*, Ginsburg correctly pointed out that, even as late as 1970, courts were still using the stereotype of woman as "keeper of the hearth"[128] to impede recognition of jury duty as a civic responsibility for all citizens, not just men.

Just as Louis D. Brandeis used a global perspective in his landmark brief in *Muller v. Oregon*, Ginsburg incorporated decisions by the West German Federal Constitutional Court (FCC) in support of her position in the *Reed* brief. The Idaho Supreme Court in *Reed* found that the legislative discrimination against women was permissible as a time-and decision-saving device in light of the fact that nature itself had established the distinction that was the basis for the discrimination.[129] The West German FCC had ruled on a similar case the decade prior to *Reed*. The statute in question, declared unconstitutional, mandated preference to the father as the representative of the child and declared that "if the parents are unable to agree, the father decides."[130] The Court's ruling, which was based on the equal protection principle of the post-World War II West German Constitution, declared that an interest in upholding the equal protection of citizens outweighed any differences in lifestyles that were alleged to exist, as well as any interest in saving time and conserving Court facilities.[131] What Ginsburg did not mention, although it was brought to her attention by a colleague, is that the German tribunal already had in place a higher standard for adjudication—something higher than what would correspond to the Supreme Court's rational basis test, but not quite strict scrutiny. Ginsburg did not develop this point further in the brief, lending itself to the theory that intermediate review, eventually appearing in *Struck*[132] and *Frontiero*,[133] was not a standard being suggested in *Reed*. She has also said that overdoing comparative side glances with foreign authorities unfamiliar to the Court would not have been wise.[134] Ginsburg included a second case from the German Court, arguing that West Germany had "relegated to the scrap heap . . . the assumption that men are better equipped than women to manage property."[135] The case concerned preference given to sons over daughters in agrarian inheritance law. Interestingly, the German Court's pronouncement was in principle only. The actual constitutional question was decided against the daughter.

In what is surely one of the most striking ironies of Ginsburg's career, the Supreme Court handed down *Reed* on November 22, 1971.[136] The same day that newspaper headlines heralded the end of bias against women,[137] the Senate Judiciary Subcommittee rejected the House-approved Equal Rights

Amendment. It is ironic because some of the Justices' conference discussions in *Reed*, and again in *Frontiero*,[138] factored in the pending ERA. Justice Potter Stewart, in particular, was known to withhold his vote in *Frontiero*, citing the possible passage of the amendment as his reason. Ginsburg, too, hoped that the ERA would accomplish—in one fell swoop—what she would eventually spend a decade working for tirelessly. Ginsburg did believe however, that the ultimate decision reached in *Reed* was consistent with judicial restraint, a principle she firmly supports. She has characterized the opinion as "terse" and referred to the decision as a "small, guarded step."[139] Ginsburg recognized that the Court was still sensitive to criticism for what was perceived as "moving too far, too fast" in the civil rights cases. Consequently, she mused, the Justices might have been reluctant to take the lead in another social reform, preferring instead to keep a careful eye on Congress's handling of the ERA.[140]

Nonetheless, siding with Sally Reed, the Court for the first time found that a state had violated equal protection in a sex discrimination case.[141] In finding the designated provision of the Idaho code unconstitutional, the Justices employed only the lowest tier of review—the rational relation test. The Court did not respond to Ginsburg's main argument in *Reed*. In the analysis of Henry Abraham and Barbara Perry, "[n]ot wisdom, fairness, intelligence, or even democracy [was] an issue: the key [was] the law's 'reasonableness.'"[142] Although the *Reed* brief was not successful in convincing the Court to adopt gender as a suspect classification, it was the initial victory for Ginsburg's litigation strategy. Although *Reed* is often seen as a natural decision on the part of the Court given the changing social climate and decisions of lower courts, it is not always assigned the full importance it deserves. The brief is rightly touted as the foundation of many legal opinions that followed concerning areas of gender discrimination. However, the most immediate impact of the ruling was the

Court's decision to include the brief's language of "substantial relation" in its unanimous opinion.

The prevailing sentiment among constitutional scholars and Court watchers is that Ginsburg's major contribution to the battle to eradicate sex discrimination was three-fold. First, the *Reed* brief laid the groundwork for the first ruling by the Supreme Court that the government had violated the Equal Protection Clause.[143] Second, she convinced four Justices that sex should be a suspect class in *Frontiero*, and third, her amicus curiae brief in *Craig v. Boren*[144] led to the enunciation of heightened scrutiny. Reexamined, the strategy actually begins with the modification of the rational basis test. Ginsburg's first actual victory was not just the acceptance of Mrs. Reed's position by the Court; it was the subtle shift in the language of the Court's opinion. No longer would the Court require a government interest be rationally related to the classification of women; now the Court would require the relation to be "substantial." This seemingly small addition was the foundation for the argument Ginsburg would make two years later in *Frontiero*.

It is unlikely that Ginsburg intended for the intermediate standard of review, or "heightened scrutiny," eventually suggested in *Frontiero*, to be proposed originally in *Reed*. The use of the term "intermediate" in the brief should not be overemphasized, given the relatively little weight assigned the idea in the text. Although the inclusion of the brief's language in the opinion was obviously a precursor to the ideas presented in *Frontiero*, the idea of an intermediate standard does not appear to have been fully developed as a part of Ginsburg's litigation strategy at the time *Reed* was argued. Given her meticulous and thorough nature, if Ginsburg had been suggesting a middle tier as a standard of review, it surely would have been developed in the brief beyond the one sentence it occupies. Rather, one can infer that in *Reed*, Ginsburg meant simply to modify the rational basis test slightly, in the form of a reversal of the burden of proof. The success of her fall-back position indicated a willingness on the Court's part to advance slowly—a willingness, one could argue, that allowed the idea of a middle tier of review to germinate in Ginsburg's mind. Those initial thoughts, combined with the events of 1972, ensured the debut of heightened scrutiny in her *Frontiero* argument.

If the *Reed* Court left unclear its reasoning for its finding of unconstitutionality of the Idaho statute, it clarified itself the next term in *Eisenstadt v. Baird*.[145] *Eisenstadt* was not a sex discrimination case, rather, it concerned reproductive freedom. The Court held that the statute in question did not satisfy any reasonable legislative purpose, thereby failing the rational relation test. The opinion included a footnote concerning *Reed* that stated, "[o]f course, if we were to conclude that the Massachusetts statute impinges upon fundamental freedoms under *Griswold*, the statutory classification would have to be not merely *rationally related* to a valid public purpose but *necessary* to the achievement of a *compelling* state interest . . . [b]ut just as in *Reed v. Reed* . . . we do not have to address the statute's validity under that test because the law fails to satisfy even the more lenient equal protection standard."[146]

From this, one can conclude that if the Idaho statute had been found necessary to achieve some compelling state interest, then the *Reed* Court would have had to face squarely the issue of whether to declare sex a suspect category. Absent this finding, *Reed* was a narrow victory, and much of Ginsburg's mission was left to accomplish.

MAKING THE CASE FOR INTERMEDIATE SCRUTINY

Since Ginsburg's days at Harvard, Gerald Gunther had been an influential person in her career. They continued to correspond and exchange ideas on the use and application of the Equal Protection Clause to sex discrimination claims. Gunther's suggestions concerning the extension of offending statutes rather than invalidation eventually formed the core of Ginsburg's arguments on that issue in *Moritz v. Commissioner*[147] and *Frontiero v. Richardson*.[148] In 1972, Gunther published a now famous article in which he examined the evolution of equal protection doctrine, analysis that proved inspirational to Ginsburg's formation of the concept of intermediate scrutiny.[149] In his article, Gunther analyzed 15 cases whose decisions came down in the 1971 term. Using these, he concluded that three patterns of Burger Court behavior were beginning to emerge: (1) The Burger Court was reluctant to expand the scope of new equal protection. (2) There was mounting discontent with the rigid two-tier formulations of the Warren Court's equal protection doctrine. (3) The Court was prepared to use the clause as an interventionist tool without resorting to the strict scrutiny language of the new equal protection.[150]

Gunther put into print what Ginsburg surely must have hoped—that *Reed* was given a closer look than what was required by the traditional rational basis test. Because Justice Burger found "some legitimacy" in Idaho's proffered objective to simplify probate protocol, and then proceeded to find the sex criterion "arbitrary," he clearly led his brethren away from the Warren mindset.[151] Warren wrote of equal protection criteria before his retirement,

> Legislatures are presumed to have acted constitutionally even if source materials normally resorted to for ascertaining their grounds for action are otherwise silent, and their statutory classifications will be set aside only if no grounds can be conceived to justify them."[152]

If Ginsburg's litigation strategy were to succeed, Gunther's analysis—that the Burger Court's "interventionist invocations" beyond the Warren mantra would continue and gain "teeth"[153]—would prove a necessary component. However, Gunther must have reined in Ginsburg's ambitions somewhat with his opinion that more vigorous scrutiny for sex discrimination did not necessarily signal application of the new equal protection doctrine.[154]

Gunther noted that Justice Marshall in the 1972 case *Police Department of Chicago v. Mosely*[155] employed a test not conforming to either old or new equal protection. Although the Burger Court refused to extend the range of suspect categories beyond those created by the Warren Court, Justice Marshall wrote for the Court that First Amendment interests were "closely intertwined," therefore the classification should be "carefully scrutinized."[156] Marshall's malaise about applying either one of the standards of review confirms Gunther's theory that the Court was becoming discontented with the rigid two-tier formula of equal protection application.[157] Herein lays the genesis of Ginsburg's incorporation of heightened scrutiny into her litigation strategy.

ONE VOTE SHY OF VICTORY: *FRONTIERO V. RICHARDSON*

The Court's swift decision in *Reed v. Reed*[158] caused Ginsburg's litigation strategy to go awry before it was even fully underway, albeit through no fault of her own. Her initial plan was to present to the Court a pair of cases, *Reed* and *Moritz v. Commissioner*,[159] to emphasize that sex role stereotyping had negative ramifications for both sexes.[160] Charles Moritz was a lifelong bachelor who, at 63, cared for his elderly mother. The Internal Revenue Code at the time allowed for never married daughters, but not never married sons, to claim a tax deduction for the cost of a nurse in such situations.[161] Ginsburg had planned to argue that even if Sally Reed was better at numbers than her husband, and even though Charles Moritz took excellent care of his mother, the State of Idaho and the Internal Revenue Service, respectively, found these facts irrelevant because the "legislature must make rules for the generality of cases, not for the exceptional instances."[162] The timing of the cases' passage through the judicial system was ill fated, rendering Ginsburg's attempt to present them as a pair to the Burger Court futile. The day the *New York Post* ran a full front-page headline declaring *High Court Outlaws Sex Discrimination*,[163] *Moritz* was still lingering after 18 months in the Court of Appeals, illustrating the difficulty in orchestrating test case litigation.[164] Eventually, Charles Moritz received his tax deduction after a favorable ruling, marking the first time a provision of the Internal Revenue Code was struck down. Despite the unsuccessful timing of *Moritz* for Ginsburg's original purpose, the case made a substantial contribution to her future efforts. In the course of the case, the Solicitor General enumerated over 800 federal laws that differentiated on the basis of sex, providing the stimulus for future test cases, among them *Weinberger v. Wiesenfeld*[165] and *Califano v. Goldfarb*[166] to name just a few. In addition, *Moritz* was an example of Ginsburg's extension argument, which she would employ successfully in her next case, *Frontiero v. Richardson*.[167]

Sharron Frontiero joined the Air Force in October 1968 for a service period of four years. In December of the next year she married Joseph Frontiero, who was a full time student at Huntington College in Alabama. The provisions of 37 U.S.C. 401 and 403 granted a housing allowance to married members living off base, with the amount varying based on the number of dependents claimed. The statute was set up to apply differently to male and female service members, allowing males to receive benefits automatically for their spouses, while females had to prove that their husbands were "one-half" dependent on them.[168] Sharron Frontiero provided one-third of her husband's support, but fell just shy of the requirement that she provide three-fourths the total family income. The District Court held that "the challenged statutes are not in conflict with the Due Process Clause of the Fifth Amendment."[169] Lt. Frontiero and her husband appealed to the Supreme Court.[170]

Frontiero was the first of six cases that Ruth Bader Ginsburg would argue before the Supreme Court. Oral argument was divided between the original Alabama lawyer, Joseph J. Levin, Jr., of the Southern Poverty Law Center (SPLC), and the ACLU. As evidenced by several letters between Levin and Ginsburg, the circumstances surrounding that final division of labor are a testament to Ginsburg's dedication to the mission of the WRP. From the outset of the collaboration between the SPLC and the WRP on *Frontiero*, there were irreconcilable differences on several matters. Ginsburg felt that appellants would do well to solicit amicus curiae briefs from the Women's Law Fund and the National Organization for Women (NOW), among others.[171] It was Levin's position that appellants should keep a good "Nixonian low profile" in a case he considered inappropriate for amicus briefs.[172] There also was deep division between the two parties on the issue of whether, and how strenuously, to argue for suspect classification as had been done in *Reed*.[173] Working with Chuck Abernathy of Harvard Law School, Levin reasoned that it was better to argue on the merits alone than challenge "the Burger Justices' preoccupation with decisions that have a revolutionary impact on the courts."[174] This severe split in strategy is reflected in the substantial differences between the appellants brief and the amicus eventually filed by Ginsburg. There was also initial disagreement on the usefulness of statistical information concerning income levels to rebut the government's rationale behind the benefit scheme, although those differences were rectified and incorporated into the final brief for the appellants.[175]

The breaking point between Ginsburg and Levin came in October 1972, a mere month before the *Frontiero* brief was due. It was Ginsburg's initial impression that upon assuming responsibility for the jurisdictional statement, the WRP would handle *Frontiero* at the Supreme Court. However, in an October 17, 1972 letter to Mel Wulf, Levin wrote that while he would like advice from the ACLU, he would serve as the oral advocate before the Court.[176] Caught completely off guard by Levin's change of mind, Ginsburg immediately responded that it was important for a woman to argue the case, and furthermore, that she was the best candidate, stating "I am not very good at self-advertisement, but I believe you have some understanding of the knowledge of the women's rights area I have developed over the past two years."[177] Levin retorted that it did not make "one iota" of difference who argued the case—male or female—and that he found himself trying to determine "exactly at what point we allowed ourselves to become assistants in our own case."[178] He concluded with the ultimatum that the SPLC would handle the case with or without the ACLU in light of the "two clients that asked us to represent them—and we shall."[179] After receiving Levin's letter, Ginsburg cancelled their next meeting, writing to Levin that he had "made [her] temperature rise," and that if all he required were suggestions, he should consult the appropriate chapter of her book.[180] Ginsburg and Wulf decided that the ACLU would file an amicus brief, to which Levin consented, although beyond that, he stuck to his original position and allowed no other parties to file.

During the exchanges between Ginsburg and Levin over *Frontiero*, Ginsburg was involved in another equal protection challenge before the Court that may have factored into her headstrong stance. The same day Levin's infuriating letter arrived, the Court granted certiorari in *Struck v. Secretary of Defense*.[181] Susan Struck was a career officer in the Air Force who challenged the government with disadvantageous treatment on the basis of sex. After becoming pregnant while stationed in Vietnam, she declared her intention to place her child up for adoption. The striking feature of Captain Struck's case was her government sanctioned option to have an abortion without any disruption of military service. Because her religious faith precluded abortion, she was notified that she would be subjected to an Air Force regulation that required that she be "terminated with the least practicable delay when it is established that she . . . has given birth to a living child."[182] Had *Struck* been heard before the Court it would have marked the first time that Ginsburg submitted a brief requesting an intermediate level of scrutiny as a fallback position to the strict scrutiny argument already articulated in the *Reed* brief.[183] However, at the end of November 1972, the Air Force granted Captain Struck a waiver and the Solicitor General successfully suggested that the case had become moot.[184]

The inability to use *Struck* as a vehicle for equal protection challenges left *Frontiero* as the only chance for a solid sex discrimination ruling that term. A third case on Ginsburg's agenda, *Schattman v. Texas Employment Commission*, had been denied certiorari.[185] Thus, in December of 1972, Ginsburg attempted to reconcile with Levin. She sent him copies of her *Frontiero* amicus brief and asked him to reconsider his position on suspect classification. Whether or not Levin was influenced by her amicus is unclear. However, his argument for the selective application of strict scrutiny in *Frontiero* parallels the reasoning of Ginsburg's intermediate scrutiny argument in *Struck*. Both arguments addressed prescriptions that worked to women's disadvantage, as opposed to statutes that claimed to operate in her favor. Such laws, they reasoned, should be subjected to elevated review. Ginsburg felt that all laws targeting women as a class should be subject to strict scrutiny, regardless of whether they were "benign," or worse, heaped further discrimination on an already disadvantaged class. While Levin had positioned himself to secure victory for Sharron Frontiero without ambitions of a broad declaration of sex as a suspect class, Ginsburg was determined to use *Frontiero* as the next step in her litigation strategy. Undaunted by Levin's refusal to cooperate with her efforts, her amicus brief builds and expands on Levin's arguments in several important ways. With respect to the specific circumstances in Sharron Frontiero's case, Ginsburg and Levin were largely in agreement. Both briefs argue that upon finding that the challenged provisions violate the Fifth Amendment, the Court should not strike down the benefit scheme, but extend to women the same benefits available to male members. Ginsburg had previously written about the choice between extension and invalidation as the remedy for discriminatory sex lines.[186] She pointed to Justice Harlan's concurring opinion in *Welsh v. United States*[187] as the blueprint for the extension route.[188] The facts of *Frontiero* provided an appropriate forum for incorporating the extension option into her litigation strategy. Depending on the court's perception of the dominant legislative purpose, she wrote, "a salvage operation may be undertaken."[189] Levin's brief complemented Ginsburg's by addressing in detail the intent of Congress in adopting the statute in question. The appellees misrepresented the original purpose, claiming that legislators were responding to the Air Force's need to attract more men.[190] In reality, the bill's sponsor intended to put the Armed Forces on a competitive basis with the private sector in order to attract as many men and women as possible into careers with the service.[191]

The appellees also defended the statute on the grounds of administrative convenience, just as the Idaho statute had been defended in *Reed*. The crux of the government's argument was that the District Court had correctly used the rational basis test in determining that the classification was constitutional. The three-judge court held that requiring actual proof from servicemen that their wives were dependent imposed too great a burden.[192] Levin's argument was based solely on facts and figures; he introduced Executive Department figures demonstrating that civilian females made a yearly average income higher than that of military males. He successfully rebutted the government's contention that their presumption of dependency was justified because women earn less than men.[193] If, as the government argued, lower income dictates dependency, the benefit scheme was not only unreasonable, it was diametrically opposed to its purported reasoning.[194] Ginsburg employed a similar argument, but went further, noting that the administrative convenience was nothing more than a cover for the stereotypical notion that the husband, whatever his income, ought to be treated as the breadwinner.[195]

The argument against administrative convenience in Levin's brief is an example of his narrow focus on attaining victory for Sharron Frontiero. He focused exclusively on the admission of the government that the classification's purpose served only to lighten the administrative workload, unlike Ginsburg who addressed the administrative convenience rationale in all its forms. Whereas Levin gives minimal attention to *Reed*, Ginsburg delves into the Burger Court's holdings on the point, citing not only *Reed*, but also analyzing *Stanley v. Illinois*,[196] where the Court declared unconstitutional legislation that was based on the administratively convenient premise that unwed fathers are neglectful parents.[197] Most importantly, Ginsburg addressed two cases on this point that Levin excluded altogether. Only two months before briefs were filed in *Frontiero*, a three-judge court in *Miller v. Laird*[198] struck down a different classification contained in 37 U.S.C. 401, the housing allowance provision that was at issue in *Frontiero*.[199] As Ginsburg pointed out, the Court of Appeals for the District of Columbia Circuit rejected the notion that administrative convenience justified the denial of medical benefits to children born to unmarried persons in the service.[200] Furthermore, while Levin was content that the dependency rules being challenged were indistinguishable from the mandatory preference rule in *Reed*, and by implication, also unconstitutional, Ginsburg took the offensive. The previous term, the Court had affirmed without opinion *Forbush v. Wallace*[201] in which a lower court weighed administrative convenience against a married woman's right to retain her birth name, finding for the state and characterizing the woman's injury as *de minimis*.[202] Recognizing that the administrative convenience argument was not fully settled in *Reed*, Ginsburg put the Court on notice that any further acceptance of administrative convenience rationale would be de facto approval of sex-role stereotyping as a legitimate basis for legislative distinction.[203] Apart from their analyses of the administrative convenience rationale and the merits of extension over invalidation of the offending statute, the briefs of Ginsburg and Levin had little in common. The parties were in agreement that the instant classification failed the rational basis test. Ginsburg attempted unsuccessfully to convince Levin to adopt her position on strict scrutiny in the event that the Court used strict review, which it had indicated was possible in *Eisenstadt v. Baird*.[204] Levin again made it clear that his goal was winning *Frontiero*, and while the WRP might "share in the benefits" of a win on the merits, the mission of the WRP was not his consideration.[205] A win based on the rational basis test might indeed have been another building block for Ginsburg's strategy, but Levin's strict scrutiny argument, if adopted, would have been antithetical to the WRP's approach.

Levin's final position was that strict scrutiny should be applied, but only to *Frontiero*. He argued for a narrow ruling that applied only to the kind of classification challenged. He wrote that it was "patently obvious" that the statutes in question were not protective legislation, as they were in *Muller*,[206] *Goesaert*,[207] and *Hoyt*,[208] and that while those decisions may not be excusable, the standard of review to apply to such legislation was "a question that need not be reached in the present case."[209] Levin made a concerted effort to remind the Court of their own distinctions between protective and burdensome legislation.[210] Furthermore, in two separate sections of the brief, Levin emphasizes that "*plaintiffs . . . contend that a sex classification needn't always be suspect.*"[211] Ginsburg faced an uphill battle, not only against the opposing counsel, but also against her supposed colleagues who had agreed to share oral argument time with her.

Similar to her strategy in *Reed*, Ginsburg incorporated historical perspective into *Frontiero*. Again quoting Thomas Jefferson and Alexis de Tocqueville, she continually sought to educate the Justices on sex discrimination beyond the facts of the case at hand. Particular to *Frontiero*, common law heritage formed the basis of the stereotype on which the statute in question was based. Blackstone explained that the very being or legal existence of a woman was suspended during marriage and that a woman was under the protection and influence of her husband. Ginsburg argued that Sharron Frontiero was fighting against a modern, government-ordained version of Blackstone's laws that assumed wives would automatically be dependent on their husbands, and therefore deserving of benefits, while the reverse case was rare. Ginsburg argued against § 403 as one of many government positions that perpetuate the image of husband as breadwinner and wife as homemaker. Levin was unconcerned about inequities arising generally from common law heritage, stating that those laws must "stand and fall on their own merits," and were not related to the case at bar.[212]

By 1973, Ginsburg had additional ammunition for her strict scrutiny argument. Arguing that the overwhelming approval of the Equal Rights Amendment signaled Congress' intent to terminate sex-based discrimination, she quoted Representative Martha Griffiths who stated on the House floor "there was never a time when decisions of the Supreme Court could not have done everything we ask today."[213] Although Ginsburg did not suggest in the text, as she did in *Reed*,[214] that the Court had fallen behind its coequal branches in protecting the rights of women, her extensive footnoting of the efforts of the President and Congress accomplished the same purpose.

Ginsburg articulated a three-fold approach for determining the appropriate standard of review. She argued: (1) that the challenged statutes established a suspect classification for which no compelling justification could be shown; (2) that if the Court did not find sex to be suspect class, or chose to defer the issue, that the Court should employ an intermediate test as developed in recent decisions, allowing for "close scrutiny" of the legislative objective; and (3) without regard to the invidiousness of the classification, that the statute failed even the established rational relation test.[215] Separating her arguments from Levin's, she emphasized that "*amicus* asks the Court to add legislative distinctions based on sex to the category of suspect classifications,"[216] and "*amicus* urges the application of an intermediate test" in appropriate parts of her brief.[217]

Although Levin held no ambitions about his case's impact on the movement for women's full equality, Sharron Frontiero was a self-titled "flaming feminist," and Ginsburg had definite plans to give the enthusiastic plaintiff a prominent place in history. Building on Levin's cut and dry analysis of the Frontiero's financial circumstances, Ginsburg extrapolated to the larger implications of the statute on non-traditional marital arrangements. She correctly pointed out that Lt. Frontiero bore an extra burden in attaining the benefits that men in her position received automatically because "by congressional mandate, [her labor was] worth less."[218] She urged the Court to move away from *The Slaughterhouse Cases*[219] view of the Fourteenth Amendment, quoting respected jurist Learned Hand, who wrote, "It is this Court's function to apply the Constitution as a living document to the legal cases and controversies of contemporary society."[220]

Although Ginsburg was not dissatisfied with Burger's opinion in *Reed* per se, she felt that the Court's refusal to respond to her carefully articulated argument on the negative impact of *Muller*, *Goesaert*, and *Hoyt* was a disappointment, and contributed to the inconsistent interpretation of *Reed* by lower courts.[221] Parties favoring the declaration of sex as a suspect class saw *Reed* as a clarion call to bring test cases, while those invested in the status quo saw an implicit rejection of strict scrutiny. As mediators in the debate, courts were equally confused. Ginsburg delineated the two mindsets, one using *Reed* to hold unconstitutional statutes such as the one challenged in *Lamb v. Brown*[222] concerning sex-age differentials for juvenile offender treatment, the other camp citing *Reed* as precedent in cases such as *Eslinger v. Thomas*,[223] which allowed a state senate to refuse to hire a female page.[224] No clear distinctions were made between statutes that were upheld and that were struck down. Notably, both subsets involved statutes regulating the termination of pregnant women, and the final decisions were contradictory. Because discrimination based on pregnancy was also a priority of the Women's Rights Project, the *Frontiero* amicus became a manifesto of sorts for Ginsburg.

Not content to be overlooked again, Ginsburg took a more aggressive approach in requesting that the courts reevaluate the "benign" classifications in the offending trilogy. This time she prefaced her argument with commentary on *Bradwell v. Illinois*[225] and *Minor v. Happersett*.[226] Again her caustic wit was revealed when she responded to Justice Bradley's "law of the Creator" line in his *Bradwell* concurrence, stating "although the method of communication between the Creator and the jurist is never disclosed, 'divine ordinance' has been a dominant theme in decisions justifying laws establishing sex based classifications."[227]

The need to address *Muller* became even more pressing by the time *Frontiero* was argued. In 1972, an Ohio court held explicitly that *Reed* did not overrule *Muller*. In addition, contemporary scholarship on the subject was growing, calling *Muller* a "roadblock to the full equality of women."[228] Ginsburg grew more aggressive in her approach toward *Goesaert* as well, writing "it was retrogressive in its day and is intolerable a generation later."[229] She again pointed out the glaring discrimination between Frankfurter's words in *Goesaert* and the Court's opinion in *Truax v. Raich*,[230] this time scolding judges who held such "antiquarian" attitudes toward women while rejecting automatically the inferiority of racial or religious groups.[231]

She finished her analysis of the trilogy with a ratcheted up assault on *Hoyt*. For those on the bench still willing to argue that volunteer jury duty was an advantage for women, Ginsburg pointed out that it was quite a disadvantage for women like defendant Gwendolyn Hoyt. Although the decision in *Alexander v. Louisiana*[232] came too late to be addressed in the *Reed* brief, Ginsburg squarely faced the issue in *Frontiero*. Comparing the decision to *Peters v. Kiff*,[233] she argued that full participation of women in community affairs was valuable, and it was the idea that deserved "protection."[234] Together, the majorities in *Muller*, *Goesaert*, and *Hoyt* sustained debilitating stereotypes, and Ginsburg knew that the long overdue declaration of sex as a suspect class was necessary to halt their perpetuation by lower courts.

Despite Ginsburg's argument for the inclusion of sex as one of the announced suspect classes, she was mindful of the Court's reasons for hesitation. Whether the individual Justices were cautious about advancing too quickly, as some feared they had done in the civil rights cases, or mindful of the pending ERA ratification by states, Ginsburg announced in *Frontiero* her request for an intermediate level of scrutiny to accommodate such hesitation. It is interesting to consider what the outcome of *Reed* might have been if Ginsburg had argued then for mid-level review. Although the Court might have adopted such a tack, it is more likely that *Reed* would have still been decided solely on the rational basis test. It appears that the events of 1972 and 1973 leading up to the consideration of *Frontiero* were timed perfectly to put in place the factors that formed Ginsburg's request. Her analysis of the applicability of intermediate scrutiny occupies only two paragraphs of the brief, almost lost between the strict scrutiny and rational basis argument, and is more of a suggestion than an actual argument in itself. She was clearly testing the waters of heightened scrutiny, unsure of the Court's response to her notion that *Frontiero* was the occasion to announce that women as a class deserved the "close scrutiny" delivered to the plaintiffs in *Bullock v. Carter*,[235] in light of the Court's decision not to even comment on her comparison of race and gender in *Reed*.

In the end, Ginsburg won Levin over, as evidenced in the joint reply brief for the appellants, which reads like a stump speech for the Equal Rights Amendment, albeit without ever mentioning it. Divided into two main arguments, Ginsburg first argued that the government had, misrepresented the decision in Reed,[236] and at times completely ignored it. Appellees implicitly urged the Court to uphold the breadwinner/homemaker stereotype, employing the myth that income-earning wives were "occasional."[237] Ginsburg was annoyed with the appellees' analysis of Reed; she stated that it was "startling to any attentive reader . . . of Reed and Shapiro v. Thompson" for the government to argue that, absent a fundamental right or a declaration of suspect classification, the administrative convenience rationale was justifiable.[238]

The second part of the reply brief makes no mention of Frontiero whatsoever. It was, rather, her commentary on sex as a suspect class, incorporating historical analysis, statistical data, and sociological insight—the powerful trio Ginsburg employed in many cases. Interestingly, appellees conceded that gender contained the primary ingredient necessary to declare it suspect: "sex, like race and national origin, is a visible and immutable biological characteristic that bears no necessary relation to ability."[239] Their defense was that racial distinctions had disfavored status in constitutional history, while sex did not, as connoted in the Congressional debates over the Fourteenth Amendment. Even before Frontiero, Ginsburg never questioned the validity of that argument, but pointed to the irony of the inclusion of alienage alongside the continued exclusion of sex, despite the obvious fact that national origin fit much less comfortably than sex within the confines of the appellees own definition of requirements for suspect status.[240]

Appellees further contended that women were not a minority; in fact they exercised substantial political power,[241] which Ginsburg promptly denounced as "substituting fancy for fact."[242] Her evidence was beyond rebuttal; she noted that no women occupied seats in the Senate, only 14 served in the House of Representatives, there were no women governors, and women comprised less than six percent of state legislatures.[243] Women held so few positions of power in politics in 1973 that Ginsburg managed to footnote them all on one page.[244]

Finally, appellees handed Ginsburg a winning rebuttal by announcing that the sharp lines between the sexes "do not express an implied legislative judgment of female inferiority."[245] Ginsburg had devoted a substantial portion of both *Reed* and *Frontiero* arguing against that very point. She expanded upon that analysis in the reply brief, arguing that opinions imposing a stigma of inferiority abounded in constitutional law, a strategy adopted from Thurgood Marshall's handling of *Brown*.[246] Citing fourteen articles from the fields of sociology and psychology, she assessed the pervasiveness of sex role stereotypes that the Court had been an accomplice in perpetuating through its approval of "benign" and "protective" legislation.[247] Women, she concluded, were more deserving of scrutiny than a "discrete and insular" minority due to their separation geographically and across class lines.[248]

Frontiero was decided 8 to 1, with Rehnquist as the lone naysayer; his dissent adopted Judge Rives' reasoning from the lower court.[249] Although the discrimination against Sharron Frontiero was recognized, the eight Justices were sharply divided on the standard of review to apply. In the end, Justices Brennan, Marshall, White, and Douglas voted in favor of applying strict scrutiny, while Stewart, Powell, Burger, and Blackmun concurred with Brennan's opinion but refused to agree to the strict scrutiny portion. The inner atmosphere of the Court during *Frontiero* is one of the best—or worst— examples, depending on one's point of view, of the least political branch engaging in high stakes politics. For all of Ginsburg's effort, there were forces working for and against her position in *Frontiero* that were beyond her control. Ginsburg knew that the possible passage of the ERA, among other issues, was a consideration in the Justices' minds, but she could not have known—indeed, she did not know until *The Brethren* was published in 1979[250]—about the wheeling and dealing being carried on behind closed doors in the marble temple.

Chief Justice Burger preferred not to assign Justice Brennan civil rights cases, but gave him the responsibility for the opinion in light of the agreed upon standard of review. Although the four liberals wanted to go further than the Court had in *Reed*, the conference agreed that maintaining the rational basis test was an acceptable compromise.[251] Despite the conference compromise, Brennan was convinced that the Court should make a statement, and circulated the agreed upon opinion with an alternate section proposing a broad conditional rule declaring sex a suspect class. White, Douglas, and Marshall signed on immediately, and Brennan courted Powell as the fifth vote. Powell was unhappy with Brennan's tactics and thought that his alternate draft read like a "women's liberation tract."[252] In addition, Powell thought the decision would be a summary judgment in light of the progress made on enacting the ERA, and circulated a concurring opinion on those grounds. He convinced Blackmun and Burger to join him in concurring, leaving Stewart as the fifth vote.

Stewart's actions in *Frontiero* represent another tragic irony of Ginsburg's career. Her ultimate goal was the full equality of men and women, preferring it to come in the form of the Equal Rights Amendment, but meanwhile laboring long and hard to achieve its equivalent in case law. Both strategies were teetering on the edge of success in January 1973. Stewart disagreed with Powell that the ERA precluded the Court from deciding *Frontiero* as originally agreed upon, but he also disagreed with Brennan's great leap forward, believing that progress should be slow and steady. He told Brennan he was *certain* the ERA would be ratified, and that if Brennan would go back to the original conference compromise, he promised his vote for strict scrutiny on the next sex discrimination case.

Otherwise, he would go on record against Brennan, making it more difficult to decide for strict review in the future. Brennan was not certain that the ERA would be ratified and wanted to make progress on the issue. He rejected Stewart's offer.[253] Of course, the ERA was never ratified, *Frontiero* came down one vote shy of a strict scrutiny victory and together, those facts created a cruel twist of fate for Ginsburg.

Frontiero was a surprise for Ginsburg, but not because the Court failed to declare sex suspect. Rather, Ginsburg thought the votes and Brennan's language in the opinion constituted a quantum leap for her litigation strategy. She felt that the Court had moved beyond *Reed* more quickly than anyone had anticipated.[254] *Reed* had only just crossed the line into equal protection analysis of sex-based classifications, and just two years later four Justices led by Brennan joined in a plurality opinion which declared that "classifications based upon sex, like classifications based upon race, alienage, or national origin, are inherently suspect, and [subject] to strict judicial scrutiny."[255]

Ginsburg declared *Frontiero* a success for her litigation strategy on four grounds. First, a plurality endorsed her plea for the application of strict scrutiny, and the fifth vote from Stewart seemed possible in the future, given his one sentence concurrence acknowledging the "invidious discrimination"[256] of the statute in question. Disappointed in Stewart's failure to announce the standard he preferred, she joked that lower courts should assume that Stewart "knows sex discrimination when he sees it, just as he knows hard core pornography when he sees it."[257] Stewart's motives became unclear following a conversation he had with students at Harvard Law in 1973, a favorite story that Ginsburg often recounts in her work. During the conversation, Stewart is reported to have ruminated over why women even want the ERA when they can attack discriminatory laws and keep the ones that favor them—in essence they could "have it both ways."[258] Hearing that comment and looking at the *Moritz* list of cases, Ginsburg recalls being depressed. It was, as she noted, a matter of perspective, as every one of the 800 odd statutes could be characterized as discriminatory or favorable, depending on point of view.[259]

Frontiero was also a victory considering its effect on statutory interpretation. While *Reed* involved an antiquated statute repealed before argument, *Frontiero* concerned an active benefit scheme reflective of a larger, more common statutory pattern. Ginsburg saw Lt. Frontiero and her husband as victims of policies that typecast men and women. Even into the 1970s, those roles were rewarded, while non-traditional roles were ignored or punished, not only in the military, but also for Social Security purposes, workmen's compensation, and disability laws.[260] Several areas of the law that the WRP aimed to target were discriminatory precisely because of legislative assumptions like the one the Court saw through in *Frontiero*. Finally, *Frontiero* broke ground by laying to rest the administrative convenience defense for states and localities, and by extending the benefits, rather than invalidating the statute, as Ginsburg had argued.[261] She felt that the use of the extension remedy was of critical importance because women were being raised to the level of men in the eyes of the law.[262]

The most troubling aspect of *Frontiero* for Ginsburg was not Rehnquist; he could always be counted on to disagree with any, much less a more stringent, equal protection analysis of sex discrimination. Rather, Ginsburg spoke out against the seeming hypocrisy of Justices Powell, Burger, and Blackmun in their concurrence, which counseled restraint against the judicial preemption of political decisions.[263] Only a month before, those same Justices displayed a much more activist attitude toward the role of the Court in the political process in *Roe v. Wade*.[264] Ginsburg chastised the Court for the inconsistent results between *Roe* and the equal protection cases she was bringing. Besides *Frontiero*, the Court's inaction in *Struck* was in direct opposition to their holding in *Roe*.

Susan Struck was almost terminated because she wouldn't

have an abortion in 1972. Ginsburg felt that the Court missed its opportunity to link reproductive choice to the disadvantageous treatment of women. She has written on the missed insight of 1973:

> First, if even the military, an institution not known for avant-garde policy, had taken to providing facilities for abortion, then was not a decision of *Roe*'s muscularity unnecessary? Second, confronted with Captain Struck's unwanted discharge, might the Court have comprehended an argument, or at least glimpsed a reality, it later resisted— that disadvantageous treatment of a woman because of her pregnancy and reproductive choice is a paradigm case of discrimination on the basis of sex?[265]

Women gained the right to choose in 1973, but not because the Court found the absence of choice to be a violation of equal protection, and not because Congress was overwhelmingly in favor of choice as it was in favor of the ERA. Rather, the Court found the right to choose implicit in the already heavily critiqued privacy right and then subjected women to the ill-conceived and limited trimester approach. In March 1993, three months before her nomination to the high bench, Ginsburg reflected on *Struck*,[266] stating, "with more time and space for reflection, however, and perhaps a female presence on the Court, might the Justices have gained [such insight]?"[267]

Returning to *Frontiero*, Ginsburg strategized a five-year plan following that decision to finally achieve strict scrutiny.[268] From the *Moritz* list, she selected two pieces of Social Security legislation that were particularly egregious. Working with her friends at the New Jersey ACLU, Ginsburg selected test cases for both sets of provisions.[269] One was *Weinberger v. Wiesenfeld*, a challenge to the child-in-care provision, providing benefits for a widow and child following the death of a wage earning husband, but not applicable to families who suffered the death of a wage earning wife and mother.[270] Second, Ginsburg targeted the old age and survivors insurance benefits drawing on a set of cases including *Coffin v. Califano*,[271] which employed a one-way dependency test similar in most respects to *Frontiero*. Her strategy was to progress from *Frontiero*, to *Weinberger*, ending with *Coffin*. However, in Ginsburg's words—"sometimes the best laid plans go awry, and this one did."[272]

CHAPTER IV
LINE HOLDING AND
RETRENCHMENT

"THE FLY IN THE OINTMENT:"[273] *KAHN V. SHEVIN*

Even though the ACLU was a large organization comprised of fairly autonomous affiliates, it remained a hard and fast rule that the national ACLU office should be consulted before a state chapter sought to initiate test litigation. Much to Ginsburg's dismay, the Florida ACLU had failed to initiate such contact before representing Mel Kahn.[274] The existence of *Kahn v. Shevin*[275] was unknown to the national ACLU until probable jurisdiction was noted in *Law Week*.

Under Florida law, widows received a property tax exemption, a benefit that Kahn, a widower, sought for himself and other men similarly situated. Despite the paltry sum— about $15 annually—Kahn argued that it was a denial of equal protection to classify the sexes in such a manner. The statute in question was yet another example of 19th century legislation enacted in accordance with Blackstone's view of married women. As her husband's ward, Florida reasoned, a widowed woman must be accorded protection and favor by the state. With the assistance of the Florida ACLU, Kahn filed his complaint for declaratory relief as a class action suit and received a favorable ruling from the Circuit Court. The Florida Supreme Court subsequently reversed that judgment.[276]

Of the six cases Ginsburg argued before the Supreme Court, *Kahn* was the only one she lost. What has been seldom discussed is that she signed onto the case reluctantly. Her motive was, of course, to achieve a victory for Mel Kahn, but realistically, her participation was necessary to minimize the damage the original Florida lawyer would have inflicted on her pattern of test cases by not following protocol. *Kahn* did not fit clearly within the confines of Ginsburg's litigation strategy due to its lack of double-edged discrimination, and she knew that a loss at the Supreme Court level would have been detrimental. Thus, Ginsburg signed on to shepherd it through its final stages despite her already overwhelming commitment to publish a book, not to mention the other ACLU test cases she had in the queue.

Ginsburg found *Kahn* to be troublesome on the merits. Writing to a colleague while composing the appellant's brief, she wrote "I'll give you a gold medal if you can suggest any route other than equal protection for widower Kahn."[277] The final product was, in fact, an equal protection argument occupying only 31 pages, although its two main grounds are concise and convincing. The crux of her argument was that a tax exemption favoring women does not aid in achieving equality, rather, it reinforces their status as the weaker sex, while simultaneously discriminating unfairly against men.[278] She first argued that historical stereotypes like the one embodied by the Florida statute continued to present obstacles to women—and men—who sought to be judged on their own merits. The sex-role typecasting that stemmed from the stereotypes was present in many forms. Unlike *Reed*[279] and *Frontiero*,[280] which presented clear discrimination against women, *Kahn* exposed both sides of the coin. What superficially posed as a protective benefit to the widows of Florida actually discriminated against men by using overbroad generalizations about economic dependency between spouses.[281] Despite the ultimate goal of proving Florida's discrimination against widowed men, the bulk of the brief was dedicated to condemning the statute as yet another legal reinforcement of women's status as the inferior sex, branding it with the special markers of Ginsburg's litigation strategy: historical analysis, statistical analysis, and condemnation of outstanding discriminatory cases like *Hoyt v. Florida*.[282]

Ginsburg argued that the outdated legislation divided the widowed population into two distinct groups, self-sufficient men and disabled women.[283] Florida reasoned that women who lost their husbands would be financially destitute, while a widower remained unaffected, perhaps even relieved of the burden of financial support of his late wife.[284] Ginsburg's first priority was to combat the antiquated logic using current statistics about the economic force women had come to represent by 1970. From 1960 to 1970, half the increase in the labor force was accounted for by married women, creating a total of almost 60% of America's working population in the form of married women—married and living with their husbands.[285] Inserting her personal style into the section on statistical analysis, she reminded the Court that half the new employees in certain jobs, notably bookkeeping and bartending, were women.[286]

Widowed women, she argued, did not constitute a clear economic class. Taking a cross-section of Florida's population not only disproved the rationale behind the statute, it actually reinforced the opposite conclusion: many women during marriage were self-supporting, making important contributions to the family unit, and often saddled with earning income to care for their ailing husbands, given the data about life expectancy.[287] In addition, there were surely affluent widows who needed a tax break far less than many of Florida's widowers. To lump all widows together as a disadvantaged class, despite the voluminous evidence to the contrary, and without regard to any biological difference between the sexes, was the very definition of an "invidious classification."[288] Moreover, when the statute was drafted, the exemption was granted to a "widow dependent on her own exertions that has a family dependent on her for support."[289] By 1895, the statute was broadened to widows "dependent on their own exertions," and by 1941, the exemption was without qualification to all widows.[290] While women were gaining opportunity elsewhere in America in various and diverse ways, those residing in Florida seemingly became needier over the course of six decades; a trend that Ginsburg felt "defied rational explanation."[291]

Having established that Florida's legislature had undertaken to draw lines between the sexes based on outdated stereotypes, she entered into an analysis of precedent. For Ginsburg, this was a standard exercise. She drew support from her hard won victories in *Reed*, *Frontiero*, and *Moritz*,[292] among others. In *Reed*, the Court struck down a classification not unlike the one challenged in *Kahn*. Chief Justice Burger wrote for the majority that "different treatment . . . on the basis of . . . sex . . . [would be] subject to scrutiny,"[293] a word normally employed only in adjudicating cases of racial discrimination. Striking back at commentators who had written in the interim that *Reed* employed nothing more than the rational basis test, Ginsburg noted that the rational basis test required judicial tolerance of a classification unless it was patently arbitrary. However, the *Reed* Court struck the statute in question as arbitrary, although the governmental interest was not without some legitimacy. The combination of such key phrases, Ginsburg wrote, suggested a departure from the two-tiered equal protection analysis, because it had no comfortable fit on either tier. To ignore the language of *Reed*, and claim it as a traditional equal protection ruling, was to turn a blind eye to the obvious testing of the waters for a new mode of equal protection adjudication.

As stated, *Kahn* was not a planned part of Ginsburg's litigation strategy, and did not present the opportunity to further her argument for an intermediate level of review. The *Kahn* brief asked for a traditional equal protection ruling, the most conservative request of Ginsburg's judicial career, yet she used the *Kahn* brief to highlight the language that she and Gerald Gunther found so telling in *Reed*. Inserted in the *Kahn* brief is a one-paragraph assessment of the impact of the *Reed* decision and its role as an indicator of changes in the Court's perspective. For the purposes of *Kahn*, a succinct analysis of *Reed* as the first decision holding a sex-based classification unconstitutional would have sufficed. The potential for the eventual declaration of sex as a suspect class bore no direct relation to the argument she made for *Kahn*, due to her simple request for the rational basis test, yet Ginsburg did not pass up the opportunity to respond to *Reed*'s detractors in print.[294]

Ginsburg's analysis of *Frontiero* in the *Kahn* brief presented an even better opportunity to highlight sex differentials in law because: (1) she felt the *Frontiero* statute had been easier for Ginsburg's opponents to justify than the statute at issue in *Kahn*, yet had been found unconstitutional, and (2) the same specific breadwinner/homemaker stereotype that was at issue in both cases had been declared constitutionally impermissible in *Frontiero*.[295] The law at issue in *Frontiero* allowed a woman to receive the benefits in question if her situation met the stated requirements, yet in *Kahn*, the law disqualified men from the tax exemption by virtue of their sex alone. Ginsburg wielded Brennan's words from the plurality opinion in *Frontiero* as if they had the force of law, reminding the Court that "the imposition of special disabilities upon the members of a particular sex because of their sex would seem to violate the basic concept of our system."[296] Furthermore, although Ginsburg did not stress the point in the *Kahn* brief, both cases concerned the standards by which government benefits were distributed, and *Frontiero* carried a much larger price tag.

By the end of 1973, Ginsburg had additional ammunition with which to fight sex-based differentials, although it came from an unlikely source. Even the conservative Nixon administration had recognized the advancements made in *Reed* and *Frontiero*, as evidenced by the statement of the Solicitor General in two pregnancy discrimination cases that "it is now settled that the Equal Protection Clause of the Fourteenth Amendment . . . does not tolerate discrimination on the basis of sex."[297] The statement carried such force because it specifically referred to discrimination *on the basis of sex*, and not just discrimination *against women*. Building on this awakening, Ginsburg built her case for sex discrimination as the double-edged sword that she and so many leading scholars had argued it was for years. Much of the feminist scholarship in the 1970s, and indeed into the modern day, is based on the notion that the struggle for women's full equality as citizens necessitates a change in mindset, not just case law. She sought the recognition that gender discrimination is an issue of human rights, not just women's rights.

Ginsburg also argued that legislative lines based on sex stereotypes were detrimental and oppressive to both genders, regardless of the motive of the legislature. She found support in *Stanley v. Illinois*,[298] the first case where such stereotypical thinking was found to be discriminatory to men. The *Stanley* Court found that although the legislative presumption at issue might hold true for a majority of cases, lumping unwed fathers into a class was a denial of due process, and thus an unconstitutional distinction. Lower courts had also begun to recognize the disparate treatment of men in a series of 1972 and 1973 cases. In the *Reed* brief, Ginsburg had lauded the California court that had decided, brilliantly in her opinion, *Sail'er Inn v. Kirby*,[299] which was the first case to find classifications based on sex inherently suspect.[300] Again, California courts had given her precedent on which to base her argument. The Tenth Circuit came through for her, holding that never married men were entitled to the parent care deduction provided by Congress for never married women that was previously denied. *Moritz* declared that tax classifications based on sex constituted invidious discrimination,[301] an idea that was eventually cited with approval in *Frontiero*. Another case, *Estate of Legatos v. Bank of California*,[302] predated Ginsburg's involvement with the ACLU, declaring in 1969, "both in their incidence and innate characteristics, tax moneys are sexless and soulless."[303] Together, these cases underscored the main point at issue between Ginsburg and Florida's attorneys, which was the motive of "legislative grace." It was an issue that the appellees briefed eloquently, and that would eventually lead Justice Douglas to hand Ginsburg her first defeat at the Supreme Court level.

Kahn was distinguished from *Reed* and *Frontiero* because the tax exemption was enacted by the legislature in accordance with this idea of "legislative grace," meaning that a legislative body could grant relief to certain classes of people who endured special hardship. This sympathetic view of society was considered altruistic, in theory, and not meant to discriminate against persons outside of the class. However, statutes enacted with legislative grace were yet another example of protective legislation reinforcing women's subordinate status. Although Ginsburg conceded that *Kahn* could be distinguished from *Reed* and *Frontiero*, she argued that legislative grace did not set *Kahn* so far apart from *Reed* and *Frontiero* as to make the exemption constitutional.

The tax exemption in *Kahn* was not unlike the jury exemption statute in *Hoyt*, another example of legislative grace, which assigned women an inferior role not every woman wished to play, and certainly no woman "benefited" from. The main issue in *Kahn* was that the exemption offered an additional dose of discrimination because Florida's legislature had withheld, as Congress had withheld in *Moritz*, a benefit from men who were more deserving financially than many of the women who were eligible. The Supreme Court had never taken on the idea of legislative grace directly, but the Court of Appeals in *Moritz* had explicitly considered the motive and found it to be unconstitutional. They held, "If Congress had desired to give relief to persons in low income brackets . . .

means were available through classifications geared to such objectives without using invidious discrimination based solely on sex."[304] Although Ginsburg probably did not expect the *Kahn* Court to give any more weight to the *Moritz* opinion than the *Reed* Court had given to the majority in *Sail'er Inn*, it was nevertheless the most advanced judicial statement at the time challenging the idea of legislative grace.

The last obstacle for Ginsburg was the analysis of two cases, *Hoyt v. Florida* and *Gruenwald v. Gardner*,[305] by the lower court in *Kahn*, which the appellees had interpreted in favor of their own position. The misinterpretation of *Reed* by lower courts in subsequent cases was aggravating to Ginsburg, as she outlined in the *Frontiero* amicus,[306] but those errors were far outweighed by the damage lower courts had wrought in the name of *Hoyt*. While working on *Kahn*, Ginsburg was simultaneously preparing *Edwards v. Healy*,[307] a case expected by many to deal the final blow to *Hoyt*. The *Frontiero* Court, to Ginsburg's delight, had severely criticized the *Hoyt* decision, and *Edwards* had occasioned the district court to declare, "*Hoyt* is no longer binding."[308] *Edwards* would be argued before the Supreme Court in late 1974. In the interim, however, the Supreme Court of Florida, in deciding *Kahn*, used *Hoyt* to conclude that classifications based on sex are constitutional insofar as they accord a privileged status to women. Rather than criticize the Florida Supreme Court for their clearly antiquated reasoning, she pointed to what she felt was an even more egregious use of *Hoyt*, *DeKosenko v. Brandt*,[309] as an example of the "exorbitant price" women pay for the special treatment they were receiving on the jury exemption issue.[310]

Feeling confident that *Hoyt* would soon be dismantled altogether, she proceeded to *Gruenwald*. *Gruenwald* involved the computation of Social Security benefits and accorded women favorable treatment over men in that calculation, allowing women to retire at the age of 62. The Florida Supreme Court cited the case in support of its holding in *Kahn*, but if *Hoyt* was barely sustainable, *Gruenwald* was all but overruled in the wake of *Reed*. Disposing of *Gruenwald*, Ginsburg reminded the Court that the decision was handed down when the guiding light for sex discrimination cases was Justice Frankfurter's sanction of a "sharp line between the sexes."[311] Furthermore, two years after *Reed*, the *Gruenwald* Court nearly reversed itself in *Green v. Waterford Board of Education*,[312] the same year that Congress eliminated the *Gruenwald* differential.[313] For any Justices who might have still considered *Gruenwald* as precedent, Ginsburg conceded that while the Social Security differential in that case served to counteract disparities and salary opportunities for women wage earners, the *Kahn* tax exemption was not tied to economic activity, and thus could not be held to the *Gruenwald* standard.[314] Ginsburg did not address any sex differentials in Social Security benefits in *Kahn*, but she would fight that battle the next term in *Weinberger v. Wiesenfeld*.[315]

Finally, a consistent theme throughout Ginsburg's litigation strategy is to politely remind the Court of current practices in the legislative and executive branches of the federal government. Like *Frontiero*, and *Reed* before it, Ginsburg used *Kahn* to outline the federal measures implemented in the wake of the government's realization that "the special treatment of women perpetuates sex stereotypes and thereby retards women's access to equal opportunity in economic life."[316] Between EEOC decisions and changes made by Congress to the United States Code, she cited 17 examples of new or amended national employment policies recognizing the detrimental effects of sex discrimination.[317] Furthermore, the majority of these changes overruled the administrative convenience rationale, and most involved extension of the benefit in question to women rather than removing it entirely as an option.

Having made a thorough analysis of *Kahn* on the merits, including assessment of lower court rulings, applicability of Supreme Court precedent, statistical analysis, historical presentation, and inclusion of national trends, it seemed that

Ginsburg had, once more, proven her case for an equal protection ruling at the Supreme Court level. This was all the more likely given that *Kahn*, on the merits, appeared to Ginsburg to be an easier case to prove than *Reed* or *Frontiero*, as well as an easier decision for the Justices to make given her request for a traditional equal protection ruling. Victory was certain, if in fact *Reed, Moritz,* and *Frontiero* were applicable and controlling in *Kahn*. However, Ginsburg met her match in the attorneys for Florida, who devoted the majority of their brief arguing, successfully, against that very proposition. The main contest in *Kahn* became who could convince the Court that their interpretation of that trilogy was correct.

Florida's case was based in traditional equal protection, conceding that women had been classified on the basis of their sex, but arguing that the classification was constitutional because of its substantial relation to a valid state interest. On the surface, it appeared that the matter was settled in *Reed*. In *Reed*, the Court based its opinion on *F.S. Royster Guano Co. v. Virginia*, which stated that "all persons [similarly situated] must be treated alike."[318] *F.S. Royster Guano* was the only case the Court cited as precedent in *Reed*, and thus the victory in *Kahn* would revolve around the correct interpretation of not only *Reed*, but also the Court's application of *F.S. Royster Guano* therein. In Ginsburg's analysis, if the Court mandated that all similarly situated persons must be treated alike, a state could not constitutionally discriminate against men who lost their spouses while providing a benefit for women in that situation. However, Florida outmaneuvered Ginsburg, showing that a closer reading of the Court's opinion in *F.S. Royster Guano* revealed a loophole for exemptions such as the one in *Kahn*, negating the use of *Reed* as precedent. The actual language of *F.S. Royster Guano* read: "The latitude of discretion [in classifications] is notably wide . . . for purposes of taxation and the granting of partial or total exemptions."[319] Despite the mandate for equal treatment to persons similarly situated, the qualifier differentiated *Reed* and *Kahn* so that *Reed* could not be considered precedent.

Furthermore, *F.S. Royster Guano* stipulated that although wider discretion is permissible in tax laws, "a discriminatory tax law cannot be sustained against the complaint of a party aggrieved if the classification appears to be altogether illusory."[320] Both sides acknowledged that the exemption was enacted to offset the gap in earning potential between the genders.

Unable to prove that the classification was illusory, Ginsburg nevertheless argued that the classification was overbroad using a thorough analysis of the data showing the rapid progress of women into the work force. In her reasoning, Florida's classification was based on an overstatement of women's inferior economic position. Florida countered with its own statistical analysis disputing Ginsburg's claim and stating that "[appellants] ignore the fact that [progress in the workforce] has not benefited women in regard to earning capacity. In reality, inequality of income is a severe and current problem."[321] Citing Department of Labor figures, Florida showed that women in 1955 had a median income that was 63.9% of their male counterparts. Rebutting Ginsburg's optimistic outlook of women's progress, the figures forecasted further discrepancies as the earning gap had widened by 1970 to leave women with a mere 59.4% of men's median income.

As with *Reed*, appellees challenged Ginsburg's analysis of *Moritz*. They contended that "a careful reading" of that opinion actually indicated support for their position, stating that the *Moritz* Court would have upheld that differential if the statute had been based on the inferior economic status of women, as in *Kahn*. On this point, Florida's position was strong—the *Moritz* Court had reasoned that because the parent care deduction was available to widowers, the benefit was not tied to women's economic status, and therefore bore no rational relationship to the classification.[322]

Having successfully turned Ginsburg's assessment of the precedential value of *Reed* and *Moritz* on its side—in some cases managing to argue convincingly that those two cases supported their position—Florida proceeded to dismantle Ginsburg's argument for the applicability of *Frontiero*. Ginsburg had argued that because a breadwinner/homemaker stereotype had been labeled discriminatory in *Frontiero*, it should also be struck down in *Kahn*. Appellees argued that despite this similarity, *Frontiero* was, at its core, a case about administrative efficiency as a defense for sex discrimination. Indeed, Brennan had written that the *Frontiero* statute was unconstitutional because the "sole purpose" of the differential treatment had been for administrative convenience.[323] The language of *Frontiero* clearly indicated that the government would have been allowed to maintain the differential, if it could have shown that money was saved, despite the fact that doing so would have reinforced the stereotype. As appellees pointed out, *Frontiero* held that in order to satisfy the demands of strict scrutiny, the government must show that it is cheaper to grant all men the stated benefit than to determine which service members actually meet the requirements and are therefore entitled to it.[324] The facts of *Frontiero* did not meet this standard. Appellees did not intend to defend the discrimination of women in the armed forces—they made this point solely to show that Ginsburg's analysis of the role the breadwinner/homemaker stereotype played in the decision was actually a secondary consideration.

Appellees were so confident in the compelling nature of the state's interest in closing the gap in economic status that they argued for the statute's constitutionality even when subjected to strict scrutiny review.[325] They maintained that even if *Frontiero* had elevated gender to the level of a suspect class, the *Kahn* tax exemption could be upheld in light of its implementation as a matter of "legislative grace." Granting the tax exemption to widows was far from achieving administrative efficiency, in fact, it represented a considerable expense to the state in lost revenue.[326] Furthermore, the gender-based classification was not simply the work of elected officials. The widow's exemption provision was actually contained in Florida's constitution, which had been ratified in 1968. In a year when the ERA was being hotly debated throughout the country, appellees noted that the exemption "was the expression of the will of the people of Florida."[327]

Given the sensitivity of Justices Stewart and Powell, who were the swing votes, to any appearance of the Court acting as super legislature, the fact that the exemption in *Kahn* was so strongly supported among Florida's citizens was a compelling point. However, Justice Douglas' conference notes indicate that the votes in *Kahn* revolved around the fact that the classification was for tax purposes. Douglas wrote, "LP [Lewis Powell] agrees with PS [Potter Stewart]—would have to tear up all tax codes to reverse this."[328] He noted his own vote as "inclined to affirm—widows are largely destitute."[329] Predictably, Chief Justice Burger found "all sorts of compelling interests for giving women favorable treatment."[330]

Judging by the conference notes, it appears that Ginsburg's arguments had fallen on deaf ears, with the exception of Justice White, who wrote a biting dissent in her favor. Justice White went so far as to make a point that Ginsburg did not—that if the tax exemption was truly for the purpose of remedying past discrimination, it should be extended to those who were members of a disadvantaged racial group or those who were unable to break out of the cycle of poverty.[331] Ginsburg's usual allies, Justices Brennan and Marshall, also issued a dissent, but it was on the grounds that the classification was over inclusive.[332] In Brennan's words, "some [widows] are rich."[333] Had the statute been tailored more narrowly, they would have voted to affirm, much to Ginsburg's dismay.

The majority opinion, written by Douglas, reads like a summation of Florida's case. In only four paragraphs, the Court affirmed the Florida Supreme Court's finding that that classification held a fair and substantial relation to the object of the legislation, incorporating the data about median income from the appellees brief; declared that *Frontiero* was decided on administrative convenience grounds and was therefore not controlling in *Kahn*; and declared that state tax laws are not automatically arbitrary because they discriminate against a certain class of individuals.[334]

Although *Kahn* was not intended as part of Ginsburg's litigation strategy, she did not expect the final opinion to take the form that it did. Two days after the decision was handed down, she wrote to a colleague, expressing her outrage. In a letter dated April 26, 1974, she wrote:

White is the only one with complete integrity, though I have some sympathy with Brennan and Marshall in their effort to avoid conflict with their probable position in *DeFunis*. Douglas' opinion is a disgrace from every point of view. I'm ashamed of Stewart for associating himself with such sloppy work.[335]

Many commentators agreed, noting in one way or another that Douglas had lapsed into the romantic paternalism that he joined in denouncing in *Frontiero*.

While composing the briefs, and throughout oral argument, Ginsburg had been concerned about the close proximity with which *Kahn* and another case, *DeFunis v. Odegaard*,[336] would be heard. *DeFunis* was scheduled for oral argument the day after *Kahn*. Marco DeFunis was a white applicant to the University of Washington's law school who challenged that the minority admission program denied his application consideration in a race neutral manner. Commiserating with the attorney for the University of Washington, Ginsburg thought the pairing "made a bad situation worse," fearing the Court would establish "too broad a corridor" for benign discrimination.[337] The attorney feared the opposite, that the Court would declare the constitution colorblind and allow no such corridor at all for race.[338] Ginsburg had carefully prepared to distinguish *Kahn* from *DeFunis* during oral argument, and was able to do so upon prompting by Justice Blackmun. She was delighted that the question came during her rebuttal time, allowing the two minutes she had prepared to devote to the issue to stretch into seven.[339]

The Court eventually declared the *DeFunis* case moot, as

Marco DeFunis would graduate from law school shortly after the term's end.[340] Nonetheless, Douglas issued a dissent rejecting compensatory classifications based on race,[341] a position Ginsburg felt was at odds with his position in *Kahn*. Ginsburg condemned his "defective vision,"[342] surmising that he should have decided both *Kahn* and *DeFunis* the other way.[343] She wondered whether he truly perceived it beneficial to women to rank them with Florida's blind and disabled—two other groups who were included in the exemption. She was reminded of Harvard President Pusey's remark at the height of the Vietnam draft: "We shall be left, with the blind, the lame, and the women."[344] However, her view of Douglas was tempered somewhat following the publication of his autobiographical work *Go East, Young Man*.[345] The financial difficulties of his widowed mother explained his view of widowhood in *Kahn* to Ginsburg's satisfaction, as expressed in a letter to Bill Hoppe, the man who originally litigated *Kahn* in the Florida courts.[346] For several years after the *Kahn* decision, she wondered whether the Justices truly perceived the effect of supposedly benign discrimination. In addition, she pondered whether *Kahn* might have been decided differently if *Weinberger*[347] had come to the Court first, but recognized that the tax issue was the main problem.

Responding to the flurry of case notes generated by *Kahn*, Ginsburg's correspondence with the note writers reveals much about her view of her own litigation strategy following the decision. Ginsburg felt that after the 1973-1974 term, the state of the law concerning gender discrimination could be "euphemistically described as muddled."[348] Shortly after *Kahn*, the Court decided *Schlesinger v. Ballard*,[349] and together the two decisions weakened expectations that *Frontiero* signaled a trend toward an intermediate level of scrutiny, or even a more stringent application of the rational basis test. Ginsburg did not participate in Lieutenant Ballard's case, but watched its progress closely, calling it "a tangled, idiosyncratic case."[350] Later, in a 1977 speech given to the Minnesota ACLU,

Ginsburg commented that she probably should have filed as a friend of the Court in order to point out that the Court should not review in isolation one facet of a large and complex scheme.[351]

Appellee Robert C. Ballard, a lieutenant in the United States Navy, was twice passed over for promotion after nine years of service and was discharged pursuant to Navy regulations. He brought suit against the Navy claiming gender discrimination because a woman in his position was allowed 13 years of commissioned service before being discharged for lack of promotion. The district court, relying on *Frontiero*, ruled in his favor, holding the differential treatment of officers based on gender to be solely based on fiscal and administrative concerns and therefore without justification.[352]

Writing for five Justices, Justice Stewart disagreed.[353] The Court upheld the Navy's discharge policy allowing women four additional years to achieve promotion before receiving mandatory discharge as reasonable in light of the decreased opportunity for women to achieve higher rank through combat and sea duty. He distinguished the statutes in *Reed* and *Frontiero* as archaic and overbroad generalizations while the policy in *Schlesinger* leveled the playing field for the men and women of the Navy. In *Kahn*, Justice Douglas authored the majority opinion, Justices Brennan and Marshall had issued a dissent, and Justice White had issued a separate dissent, yet in *Schlesinger* these four combined to dissent. Justice Brennan wrote that *Frontiero* focused on the difference in treatment accorded women and men, not upon the Government's interest in determining benefits, and he concluded, referring to *Kahn*, that "the Court goes far to conjure up a legislative purpose which may have underlain the gender based distinction here attacked."[354]

After the *Kahn* decision, one student wrote to Ginsburg that he was optimistic that the four Justices in *Frontiero* would find a fifth vote and declare sex suspect. He asked specifically how Justice Blackmun could be persuaded to become the fifth vote. Ginsburg did not respond to his inquiry about Blackmun, but she did indicate that *Kahn* was "the fly in the ointment" of her litigation strategy, and that five votes for strict scrutiny in her next challenge was unlikely.[355]

THE "PREGNANT PROBLEM"

Kahn v. Shevin[356] was argued in January 1974 and decided in April of that same year.[357] During this period, Ginsburg and her ACLU colleagues were participating as amicus in a set of challenges to the treatment of pregnancy in the workplace. Over the next three years, the Court heard five cases on this issue, none of which advanced the equal protection argument Ginsburg made on the plaintiff's behalf.

In October 1973, the Court heard arguments in a pair of consolidated cases, *Cleveland Board of Education v. LaFleur* and *Cohen v. Chesterfield County School Board*, to determine if mandatory maternity leave at a fixed point in pregnancy violated the rights of public school teachers.[358] A year prior, Ginsburg authored the brief for the petitioner in *Struck v. Secretary of Defense*, which discussed in detail the constitutional issues raised by mandatory leave requirements due to pregnancy.[359] Because *Struck* was mooted before the Court was able to adjudicate the issues involved, *LaFleur* was the first case heard by the Court on this issue.

In Cleveland, Ohio, and Chesterfield County, Virginia, the school boards required pregnant teachers at a fixed point in their pregnancy to submit notice of their condition and take maternity leave. This allowed the school board an opportunity to plan for the employee's departure in advance, so as to avoid the interruption of the classroom environment, and ensure adequate instruction to the students, as it was assumed that the late stages of pregnancy rendered a woman unable to perform her duties adequately. In addition, both school systems required certification of fitness by a woman's physician before she was able to return to her post. The

Cleveland policy also stipulated that a woman was ineligible for rehire until the child was three months old.[360]

Ginsburg began her brief by arguing that discrimination based on pregnancy is sex discrimination even though "it can't happen to a man."[361] Sex discrimination, she offered, exists when a defined class of people, in this case women, are subjected to disadvantaged treatment based on stereotypical assumptions that operate to foreclose opportunity determined by individual merit. She noted the lower court opinion in *LaFleur*, which stated that "male teachers are not subject to pregnancy, but they are subject to many types of illnesses and disabilities."[362] The school boards in question had not seen fit to protect classes of individuals who suffer from either high blood pressure or heart conditions, calling into question their motive for the need for advance planning in the face of a possible disruption of teaching ability. In addition, Ginsburg identified the underlying assumption that such policies operated benignly in favor of pregnant women, which in operation served to curtail women's economic opportunities. By imposing an "iron rule" dealing with all pregnancies in "an identical, dehumanizing fashion," the school board deprived pregnant teachers of the equal protection of the laws.[363]

After a summation of *Reed*[364] and *Frontiero*,[365] Ginsburg turned her attention to recently decided Supreme Court cases, *Roe v. Wade*[366] and *Doe v. Bolton*,[367] arguing that a constitutional right for a woman to determine whether or not to terminate a pregnancy requires that her decision be free from the threat of forced unemployment.[368]

As with *Struck*, Ginsburg had attempted to bring this particular set of issues to the Court in a previous term. She had previously worked on behalf of Mary Ellen Schattman, an employee of the Texas Employment Commission (TEC), who was forced to leave her position in the seventh month of her pregnancy in accordance with their stated practice. Ginsburg filed the petition for certiorari, which was denied.[369] However, inspired by Schattman's comments on the anomaly of providing "free access to abortion while placing impediments in the way of the woman who wants to bear her child," ACLU personnel researched and published a paper entitled *The Right to Be Pregnant*.[370]

On behalf of Schattman, Ginsburg had argued that the Court's refusal to face the issue of the "rights of pregnant women created a very real threat of economic blackmail."[371] Although the *Schattman* petition was denied, the Tenth Circuit took the same issue under consideration the next year in *Buckley v. Coyle Public School System*,[372] and held that mandatory maternity leave "invaded privacy by requiring a teacher to choose between employment and pregnancy."[373] Citing *Buckley* in her *LaFleur* amicus, Ginsburg argued that despite the absence of a right to public employment, a woman does have the right to be free from unconstitutional conditions in connection with her employment.[374]

On January 21, 1974, the Court, ignoring the equal protection argument, decided on behalf of Susan Cohen and Jo Carol LaFleur, in a 7-2 decision holding that the mandatory maternity leave imposed by both school boards violated the Due Process Clause of the Fourteenth Amendment.[375] Writing for the seven-member majority, Justice Stewart called the cut off dates for determining leave "arbitrary," and found the Cleveland three-month return provision to be "both arbitrary and irrational."[376] The majority of the Court wholly declined to use equal protection analysis rather than due process framework for the determination of the outcome. Justice Powell, however, wrote that he was unable to join the majority opinion because of this analysis, although he did concur in the result. Whether or not Ginsburg's equal protection argument was influential in Powell's thinking is unclear. In his concurrence, it is clear that Justice Powell's reasoning parallels Ginsburg's concerning the classification of pregnant teachers for policy purposes, which he found to be "counterproductive or irrationally over inclusive."[377] Unlike Ginsburg, Powell found that applying a standard of review higher than rational basis was unnecessary as the policies in question could easily be discarded under traditional rational basis standards of equal protection. Equal protection analysis was the focus for the next in the series of cases concerning societal and governmental treatment of pregnant women. Again writing as a friend of the Court in conjunction with the National Organization for Women and the Center for Constitutional Rights, Ginsburg argued that excluding disabilities related to pregnancy from California's disability program constituted a sex classification and that it kept a woman from exercising her fundamental right to decide whether or not to bear a child.[378] In the case before the Court, four women brought suit against California alleging discrimination in violation of the Equal Protection Clause.[379] Under the California disability insurance program for private employees, each employee contributed part of his salary, and the program was structured to maintain solvency by covering specific claims, and for fixed periods of time. Disabilities not covered were those resulting from court commitment as a dipsomaniac, drug addiction, sexual psychosis, or disabilities attributable to pregnancy. Of the four plaintiffs, three women experienced abnormal pregnancies and one, Jacqueline Jaramillo, experienced a normal pregnancy that was the sole cause of her disability claim. Following a District Court ruling for the plaintiffs,[380] the administrative guidelines were revised to cover abnormal complications and three of plaintiffs' cases were mooted when their disability claims were paid. The remaining plaintiff, Jaramillo, continued to press her case and the Supreme Court granted certiorari to consider whether it constituted invidious discrimination to deny insurance benefits to women with disabilities arising from normal pregnancy and child birth.

Jaramillo's case, *Geduldig v. Aiello*,[381] was argued two months after the decision in *LaFleur*. Counsel for Jaramillo, in addition to the amicus brief Ginsburg filed, argued that California's disability program burdened the fundamental right to decide whether or not to bear a child and requested analysis under the strictest equal protection standards of review. They attempted to build on the momentum of *LaFleur*, in addition to *Roe* and its progeny that recognized rights surrounding child bearing, and stressed that the Court had not yet reached the question of the treatment of physical characteristics that were necessarily sex-based under the equal protection clause of the Fourteenth Amendment.[382]

This time the Court did entertain equal protection arguments but sided with appellants, issuing a 6-3 opinion in June 1974 holding that the state was not required to sacrifice the self-supporting nature of the program to insure participants against what the majority termed just another risk of disability, such as a normal pregnancy.[383] In a dissent joined by Justices Douglas and Marshall, Justice Brennan chastised the majority for its retreat from the apparent move to treat gender based classifications with a higher standard than traditional equal protection as it had signaled in *Reed* and *Frontiero* without an explanation as to why the classification at hand differed from those previous cases. He went on to warn "the Court's decision threatens to return men and women to a time when . . . classifications treated differently members of a particular sex solely because of their sex."[384] Following the two decisions in *LaFleur* and *Geduldig*, it appeared that the battle over pregnancy classifications was a draw, although to Ginsburg, Douglas likely redeemed himself after his *Kahn* decision by joining the *Geduldig* dissent. Although she never spoke about Douglas directly in connection with his actions in *Geduldig*, she later remarked that in that case, the Court had returned "a decision that was impossible to rationalize as a favor to women,"[385] which was possible speculation on why Douglas could be in the majority in *Kahn* and dissent in *Geduldig*.

October Term 1974 came and went without any further commentary from the Justices on what Ginsburg called the "pregnant problem," but by the spring of 1975, the ACLU was again preparing to sway the high Court on the issue. The Women's Rights Project signed on to represent Mary Ann Turner in her challenge against the Utah Department of Employment Security.[386] Although Ginsburg did not argue the case at the Supreme Court level—in fact, no argument was necessary as the case was decided without argument—she played a major role in drafting the appellant's brief.

Turner was fired from her job for reasons unrelated to her pregnancy and subsequently filed for unemployment compensation. She received benefits from the state until 12 weeks prior to her expected delivery date in accordance with the Utah provision that disqualified pregnant women from receiving payment from that given point until six weeks after childbirth. Turner had taken her case to the Utah Supreme Court, which found no violation of constitutional guarantees, although it failed to give explicit consideration to a possible violation of due process.[387] In drafting Turner's petition for certiorari, Ginsburg was mindful of the outcome of *LaFleur*, but in a strategic move, decided not raise the failure of the lower court to consider due process issues. In a memorandum to fellow WRP counsel, Kathleen Peratis, Ginsburg advised "It's not a reason for granting cert., but might be a reason for Burger and Blackmun to argue against taking the case."[388] In addition to Burger and Blackmun, Ginsburg was conscious of the policy preferences of Justice Stewart, who authored the *LaFleur* opinion, and constructed her due process argument in line with what she felt would appeal to him.[389]

Based on *LaFleur*'s outcome, Turner's case was strong, and was boosted by the unfortunate decision of Utah's counsel to attempt to argue that their case should be decided based on *Geduldig* rather than *LaFleur*. Utah had argued in state court that their statute was based on "employability." After the high court declared this rationale a violation of due process in *LaFleur*, Utah argued against granting certiorari in *Turner v. Department of Employment Secretary of Utah*[390] by asserting that its rationale was not based on employability, but on the exclusion of risks. *Geduldig* had upheld a California unemployment insurance program that was based on the exclusion of risks. It is unlikely that the Court needed Ginsburg to point out this last minute switch, but Ginsburg did capitalize on Utah's mistake, and requested clarification by the Court on whether *LaFleur* or *Geduldig* controlled the rights of pregnant women who remain fit and able to be employed. *Turner* was handed down per curiam on November 17, 1975. Ginsburg was successful in her request for clarification—the Justices held that *LaFleur* was controlling.[391]

Over the next two years, the Court heard arguments in the last two of the five cases concerning the "pregnant problem" that Ginsburg would participate in during her tenure with the Women's Rights Project. In October 1976, the Court took up the matter of the treatment of pregnant women under Title VII in *General Electric Company v. Gilbert*,[392] and then again in a follow up case, *Nashville Gas Company v. Satty*,[393] in December 1977. The ACLU signed on as amicus in Gilbert's case, a class action suit brought by a group of women challenging the disability plan of their employer that excluded disabilities arising from pregnancy in their benefits scheme. The features of the plan were nearly identical to those at issue in *Geduldig*, but the case was initially filed in the Eastern District Court of Virginia, and decided in favor of the plaintiffs, alleging discrimination in violation of Title VII of the Civil Rights Act of 1964. After the decision was handed down in *Geduldig*, the Court of Appeals affirmed *General Electric*, finding that *Geduldig* was not applicable in *General Electric* because of the Title VII context. The Court took up the case shortly thereafter, in what seems to have been a clear move to clarify that whether in the context of the Equal Protection Clause or Title VII, exclusion of pregnancy disability benefits from any benefit scheme was not gender-based discrimination.

Ginsburg had hoped to regain ground lost after the decision in *Geduldig* by the invoking of Title VII, and felt that the

Justices' unwillingness to do so in *General Electric* yielded the movement a major setback.[394] Not to be overlooked as part of her overall strategy, Ginsburg's amicus gave an exhaustive analysis of the differences between sex discrimination under the Fourteenth Amendment and its treatment under Title VII. Her strategy was to show the Justices that a gender-based discrimination claim was stronger under Title VII because Title VII addressed matters of sex and race discrimination with "equal vigor." The Constitution, on the other hand, did not, and the Court still used different standards for their adjudication even after her many years of trying to convince them otherwise. However, the Court never reached the merits of Ginsburg's argument, having decided that excluding pregnant women was not discriminatory to begin with. The consolation prize was *Nashville Gas Co. v. Satty*, which involved another Title VII challenge, this time against a company practice which denied employees both their seniority accumulated during maternity leave and their compensation during that period.[395] The Court agreed in part with the District Court which found both rules in violation of Title VII, striking down the seniority policy, but stating that the compensation policy was not a per se violation.[396] The Court remanded the case to determine whether the pay policy was "designed to effect invidious discrimination."[397]

In the two years following this set of cases, Ginsburg wrote and spoke publicly about the seeming inconsistency of the treatment of pregnant women by the high court. Quite often she reminded her audiences of the old adage about jurists which states "if two things are inextricably tied to each other and you can think of one without thinking of the other, you have a legal mind."[398] The Justices, she explained, had just such a mind when it came to pregnant women, illustrated by what she felt was their inability to see the treatment of a pregnant woman as a piece of the larger equality struggle. The overt reasoning, she thought, appeared to be the Justices' willingness to side with pregnant women seeking redress in cases where violations of due process could be shown. Alleged equal protection violations, however, could not pass muster.

She concluded that in addition to the Justices expressed opinions in the cases that came before the Court, that there might have been extrajudicial factors at work. In her words, "Perhaps the able pregnant woman seeking only to do a day's work for a day's pay is a sympathetic figure before the Court, while a woman disabled by pregnancy is suspect."[399] Parenthetically she pondered the Justices' question as whether a pregnant plaintiff is "really sick or recovering from childbirth or is she malingering so that she may stay 'where she belongs'— at home with baby?"[400] Justice Stevens aptly described the state of the law concerning the pregnant problem after *Nashville Gas* in his concurrence. Often repeated by Ginsburg, Stevens summarized that when the Court is asked to decide if disadvantageous treatment of pregnant women violates a prohibition against sex discrimination, the Court's answer should be "always," after *General Electric* the answer was "never," and the current answer was clearly "sometimes."[401] Although not completely disappointed in the Court's pronouncements concerning the pregnant problem, Ginsburg had hoped to raise the level of consciousness of the Justices with her detailed treatment of the women's situations in her briefs. Despite her inability to gain equal protection ground in any of the cases, she expressed hope following *Nashville Gas* that both the courts and the lawmakers would begin to recognize the interrelationships between all reproductive freedom matters and treat them as equality issues by the 1980s.[402]

CHAPTER V
BACK ON TRACK

The first half of 1975 yielded several important victories for the Women's Rights Project under Ginsburg's leadership. Up until that time, the progression of Ginsburg's strategy to achieve strict scrutiny of sex-based differentials in the law, and even the lesser goal of raising the consciousness of the nine men who occupied the bench, had been akin to the saying "two steps forward, one step back." However, 1975 was a banner year in terms of the WRP mission. With the virtual overruling of *Hoyt v. Florida*,[403] the four cases that the WRP set out to overturn had all been relegated to what Ginsburg referred to as the constitutional scrap heap. In addition, 1975 saw the first and last decision in which Justice William Rehnquist sided with Ginsburg in a challenge to a gender classification.

WOMEN AS JURORS: OVERTURNING *HOYT V. FLORIDA*

The first in the series of 1975 victories for Ginsburg was a case initiated by the Louisiana Chapter of the ACLU challenging the "volunteers only" provision for women in the state's jury selection system.[404] The provision automatically excused women from jury duty unless they went to their local courthouse and volunteered. The system in question mirrored the Florida system upheld in the 1961 *Hoyt* decision. Although Louisiana was the last state to hold on to that particular type of jury selection process as it pertained to women, as Florida had changed its rule a few years before, several other states including progressive New York allowed women to be excused from duty without explanation. Massachusetts excused women who found the subject matter of the trial embarrassing, and nine other states including California exempted women who asked to be relieved in order to care for their children. As described by Ginsburg in her brief for the appellees, *Edwards v. Healy*[405] was initiated by three separate classes of plaintiffs: females eligible for jury duty whose exclusion typed them as second class citizens, males eligible for jury duty whose requirement to serve constituted a burden because of the exclusion of females, and female litigants in civil cases tried in state court who were denied the possibility of receiving a jury representing a fair cross section of the community. Cases involving Spanish Americans, atheists, and laborers had been heard throughout the 1960s in appellate courts around the nation, and had established the principle that it was a denial of equal protection to exclude identifiable segments of the community. Ginsburg argued that the jury selection system invidiously discriminated on the basis of sex because women made up 53% of Louisiana's population in 1974, which certainly qualified them as an identifiable segment of the community.

Ginsburg's argument in *Edwards* focused on the first class of plaintiffs, who she claimed were being "kept in their place" by the benign discrimination practiced by Louisiana.[406] Both *Reed*[407] and *Frontiero*[408] concerned assumptions made by the state that amounted to gross generalizations about the natural place of men and women in work and home life. Just as the government assumed that Joseph Frontiero would prefer to work outside of the home, Louisiana assumed that its women citizens would prefer to not only work at home, but to be anywhere but in a courtroom. Ginsburg labeled this mode of thinking "an outgrown dogma."[409] Quoting the decision in the 1946 case *Ballard v. United States*,[410] she reminded the

Court that they had held nearly 30 years before that "the two sexes are not fungible . . . a distinct quality is lost if either sex is excluded. The exclusion of one may indeed make the jury less representative of the community than would be true if an economic or racial group were excluded."[411] In addition, she reasoned that the decision in *Hoyt* was impossible to reconcile with the recent advances made in *Reed* and *Frontiero*. Appealing once again to the *Frontiero* plurality, she reminded the Court that it had a duty to deny any practice that relegated women "to inferior legal status without regard to their capabilities." She concluded that for the Court to side with Louisiana would be to turn a blind eye to the fact that "jury service, more than voting, is not only a right, it is a crucial citizen responsibility."[412]

Edwards v. Healy was argued at the Supreme Court in conjunction with another case challenging the Louisiana system. *Taylor v. Louisiana*[413] was not initiated by the ACLU but was assisted by Ginsburg when it reached the Court. Billy Taylor had been sentenced for aggravated kidnapping by a jury that was composed exclusively of men. With court assigned counsel, Taylor had brought suit alleging a violation of his Sixth Amendment right to a fair trial because of the exclusion of women from his jury. The Court heard both cases on October 16, 1974, but handed down the decisions separately. On January 21, 1975, the Supreme Court reversed the conviction of Billy Taylor on the grounds that his Sixth Amendment right to a fair trial had indeed been violated by a jury selection system which did not disqualify women from jury service, but operated in a way that had the impact of drastically lowering the number of women available for jury service. Because states are bound to uphold the Sixth Amendment rights of its citizens by virtue of the Fourteenth Amendment's application of the Bill of Rights to state law, Billy Taylor's rights under the Fourteenth Amendment were, in due course, violated as well. Writing for the majority that included all the Justices except the lone dissenter, Justice Rehnquist, Justice White did not specifically mention the facts at issue in *Edwards*, but was sufficiently persuaded by Ginsburg's argument for the applicability of *Ballard v. United States*[414] as to include it in his opinion. Justice Rehnquist, on the other hand, felt that the opinion "smack[ed] more of mysticism than of law,"[415] and he could not detect the reason for the "swing of the judicial pendulum" in the 13 years since the *Hoyt* ruling.[416]

In anticipation of the Supreme Court's probable ruling, Louisiana lawmakers convened a special session in August 1974. They proposed a repeal of the portion of the Louisiana Constitution mandating the jury selection provision for women, which was ratified and took effect December 31, 1974. Based on this action, counsel for the State of Louisiana submitted a supplemental brief asking the Court to declare *Edwards* moot.[417] Ginsburg also filed a supplemental brief asking the Court to deny their request. She reasoned that the case could not be mooted just because the Louisiana Constitution had been revised. Although the "volunteers only" provision was stricken from the new constitution, Article V of the new document still granted the legislature authority to provide additional qualifications for jurors, an opening which Ginsburg felt made the recurrence of the discrimination real. None the less, the Court remanded the case for consideration of a mootness dismissal. The lower court dismissed the case citing the constitutional reforms.

Four years after *Edwards* and *Taylor*, Ginsburg participated in another jury exemption case, this time in Missouri. The jury selection provision in Louisiana did not place women on jury rosters initially, but allowed them to volunteer. *Duren v. Missouri*, on the other hand, concerned that state's policy of including women initially, but allowing them to decline to serve.[418] Ginsburg agreed to participate in the case and shared the oral argument with Missouri's public defender, Lee Nation. As in *Taylor*, the challenge to the jury selection system was based on the violation of a defendant's right to a jury representing a fair cross section of the community. Although the Louisiana system resulted in approximately 1% of women registered available for duty, Missouri's system increased the percentage slightly, to 15%. Missouri, led by Missouri Attorney General John Ashcroft, argued that their system and its difference in resulting percentages did not therefore operate to exclude women from service. Thus, they argued, *Taylor* was not applicable. The Court disagreed, and with an 8-1 decision in January 1979, found that indeed, the Sixth and Fourteenth Amendment rights of Billy Duren had been violated.

Ginsburg capitalized on the win in *Duren*, sending instructions to the ACLU chapters in the remaining states with similar jury selection provisions to initiate campaigns for legislative change. She included states that allowed women exemptions for child care reasons only. She was optimistic that legislative revision would be effective, but advised that beyond that, it would be necessary to try and locate a man with child care responsibilities who would probably be denied the child care exemption as mothers taking child care exemptions might not constitute substantial underrepresentation.[419] In addition, she urged the Justice Department, through Assistant Attorney General Drew Days, to initiate a change in policy in federal district courts that retained similar exemptions.[420]

As a set, the *Edwards, Taylor*, and *Duren* opinions were not the grand pronouncements on sex discrimination that Ginsburg hoped for, nor were they an aid to her goal of achieving strict scrutiny review for laws that made classifications based on gender. They were, however, the final blow to *Hoyt*, which was the last of the four decisions Ginsburg indicated she was dedicated to overturning when she founded the Women's Rights Project in 1972. Having completed that facet of the WRP's mission, she could now turn her full attention toward challenging discriminatory aspects of the law that evolved when women entered the workforce in record numbers in the middle of the century.

"A CASE NEAR AND DEAR TO MY HEART:"[421]
WEINBERGER V. WIESENFELD

The 8-1 *Frontiero* decision struck down the breadwinner/
homemaker stereotype, the most common gender line found
in federal and state legislation.[422] The government conceded
that the Court's finding meant little additional cost burden
because of the few women serving in the armed forces in 1973.
The Solicitor General warned the Court, however, that nearly
identical gender lines were used in determining Social Security
benefits, and that the equalization of those provisions would
cost hundreds of millions of dollars.[423]

Ginsburg agreed that the stakes were higher. During the
same time that she was battling Joseph Levin of the SPLC
over control of the *Frontiero* case in 1972, she was
simultaneously litigating on behalf of a widower and his infant
son in New Jersey. Throughout the *Frontiero* preparation and
argument, her strategy was to first challenge dependency tests
in the armed forces, and then attack Social Security
inequalities on a broader basis using the *Frontiero* victory.
Cases decided before *Weinberger v. Weisenfeld*,[424] however,
dampened her spirits. Ginsburg referred to *Kahn*,[425]
Geduldig,[426] and *Schlesinger*[427] as decisions indicating
retrenchment, or at best, line holding. After *Frontiero*, but
before the 1974 back steps, Ginsburg was confident that the
Court would eliminate the inequalities in government benefits
for the late Paula Wiesenfeld as it had for Sharron Frontiero.
Yet the government developed an additional line of defense
based on *Kahn*, and when *Weinberger* reached the high Court,
which precedent would rule was the question everyone—
Ginsburg included—was asking.

The Wiesenfeld family circumstances came to Ginsburg's
attention as a result of a letter to the editor written by Stephen
Wiesenfeld five months following the death of his wife in June
1972. For the seven years prior to her passing, Paula Wiesenfeld
was a public school teacher in New Jersey. Her husband,

Stephen, played the role of homemaker and became the primary caregiver to their son Jason after she died in childbirth. It was Mr. Wiesenfeld's misfortune to discover after her death that he and his son could not collect the benefits of the money she had paid into Social Security, for which a widow and child in their situation would be eligible.

Ginsburg commenced action in federal district court in New Jersey,[428] explaining to Wiesenfeld that appeals in his type of case go directly to the Supreme Court.[429] Although Ginsburg was the author of the *Weinberger* brief,[430] the attorney named in the case was Jane Lifset, a former student of Ginsburg's at Rutgers University, who was employed in a Newark firm. Following the *Frontiero* decision, the prospect for victory in Wiesenfeld's suit in federal district court looked bright. Ginsburg and Lifset immediately supplemented their brief based on Brennan's opinion in *Frontiero*.[431] In a May 1973 letter to Lifset, Ginsburg wrote, " . . . the decision pulls the rug out from under any tenable argument the [government] could make. Brennan's opinion is a joy to read!"[432]

In the supplemental brief to the district court,[433] Ginsburg compared the significance of the *Frontiero* decision to that of *Brown v. Board of Education*,[434] quoting Brennan's statement that what aligns gender "with the recognized suspect criteria, is that the sex characteristic frequently bears no relation to ability to perform or contribute to society."[435] Ginsburg believed that *Frontiero* sent a clear message that law sanctioned stereotypes failed to account for the growing number of men and women who did not "organize their lives" around such an antiquated assumption. Furthermore, the circumstances of Sharron Frontiero's case were more defensible by the government, but the Court decided against them. The differential in *Weinberger*,[436] she explained, was even more egregious than the differential declared unconstitutional in *Frontiero*. In the previous case, the husband could prove dependency, but in the case at hand, dependency of a man on his wife was not even an issue to legislators.

The government's arguments against Stephen Wiesenfeld ran the gamut of constitutional law. They argued, among other things, that extending the benefits sought to widowed fathers amounted to legislating a new class of beneficiaries which, in turn, amounted to encroachment upon the powers of Congress.[437] They disposed of *Moritz* on this basis, stating that the Court had simply reread the exemption to include men, and that this action did not require additional funding from the Treasury. They played down *Frontiero* as having very little practical effect on government spending—in their estimates it amounted to an extra percent of what had been allocated.[438] Ginsburg would eventually have to worry about the government's case built on *Kahn*, but at the time of oral argument in district court, *Kahn* had only just been granted certiorari, and the government's only similar precedent was the apparent approval with which *Gruenwald v. Gardiner*[439] had been cited in *Frontiero*.

To diffuse Ginsburg's comparison of *Frontiero* to *Brown*, the government concentrated on the cases that followed *Brown*. They attempted to compare rulings that allowed the use of race in making decisions, so long as the use of race as a factor went toward the ultimate goal of bringing the races together.[440] Their analogy was that although women were indeed entering the workforce at a rapid rate, the need of mother's benefits was still very real, and that classifications that would otherwise be impermissible, were in such circumstances warranted to achieve equality in the long run. The government quoted from a race case illustrating their analogy. In *Norwalk Core v. Norwalk Redevelopment Agency*,[441] the Second Circuit noted: "What we have said may require classification by race . . . . Where it is drawn for the purpose of achieving equality it will be allowed, and to the extent it is necessary to avoid unequal treatment by race, it will be required."[442] Finally, the government argued, as Florida's attorneys did in *Kahn*, that even if sex were elevated to the level of a suspect class, the benefit scheme was still constitutional. Despite the government's efforts to get the Court to view the cases following *Frontiero* in the manner they considered the cases following *Brown*, the New Jersey District Court did not agree.

Ginsburg worried about the conservative composition of the New Jersey court hearing Wiesenfeld's complaint, but nevertheless won the case in December 1973,[443] commenting to Lifset that it was a "weird opinion . . . [and] a minor miracle we prevailed without a dissent."[444] Ginsburg's labeling of the district court's opinion as "weird" most likely stems from the Court's commentary on the state of equal protection law after *Frontiero*. Although the Court noted that plurality opinions do not make law, and thus they would not consider any intermediate level of review for the classification in question, they went on to say that they did not even "discern" any shift in standards, dismissing outright any speculation on the language Chief Justice Burger used in *Reed*, and rejecting any cases which adopted such standards. In their view, the Court's action in both *Reed* and *Frontiero* stemmed from a pragmatic attempt to view gender classification in a modern light rather than in "stereotyped generalizations of the Victorian age."[445]

Despite all this rhetoric, the district court went on to consider exactly what they said they would not. They found that although § 402(g) satisfied the traditional equal protection test by being rationally related to a public purpose, in this case Congress' desire to alleviate the burden on women of unequal income. This rationale violated the equal protection component of the Fifth Amendment when held to a higher standard. "We are persuaded by the opinion of Mr. Justice Brennan in *Frontiero* that sex is 'inherently suspect,'" they stated, and proceeded to cite with approval a lengthy portion of Brennan's plurality opinion.[446] In light of the clear contradiction between the first and second parts of the district court's opinion, it appears that Ginsburg's use of the term "weird" to describe its composition was perhaps too generous. In the end, the Court granted summary judgment for Stephen Wiesenfeld and declared the benefits to be paid retroactively.[447]

As expected, the government appealed to the Supreme Court and the case was handed over to the Solicitor General's office, a position at the time occupied by Robert Bork, the ill-fated 1986 Reagan nominee to a Supreme Court vacancy. Due to delays by the government, the case did not reach Bork's office until February 24, 1974, the same day that oral argument in *Kahn* was heard. Ginsburg apologized to Wiesenfeld for the delay, but advised him that if *Kahn* was decided in her favor, that the Court might be persuaded to affirm the decision in his case "without further ado."[448] To Ginsburg's dismay, more delaying tactics from Bork's office ensued and probable jurisdiction in *Weinberger* was not noted until October 1974, with oral argument set down for January 1975.[449]

A critical component of Ginsburg's litigation strategy was the coordination of amicus briefs for the cases on which she was the primary attorney. In most cases, she was contacted first by the groups wishing to file as amicus, but after consenting to the filing she would mentor the authors of the briefs to ensure that their arguments meshed with hers. In *Weinberger*, she worked closely with Elizabeth Schneider of the Center for Constitutional Rights (CCR) based in New York City. She advised Schneider to include an argument for strict scrutiny application in the CCR amicus brief although the ACLU brief did not make a similar argument. She complimented Schneider on the final draft, remarking that the "amicus [was] just right. It effectively spotlight[ed] the core issue with appropriate force and supplie[d] the focus needed to compliment the ACLU brief."[450] This comment reveals Ginsburg's increasing seasoning as a political player. She did not raise the issue of strict scrutiny in *Kahn*, asking only for the application of the rational basis test, and continued to urge the Court to employ an intermediate level of scrutiny in the cases following *Kahn*. It is noteworthy that she even appeared to dodge the question of an applicable standard in later cases concerning Social Security differentials. It appears that while she was scaling back her own requests to meet the Justices half way, she nevertheless urged outside groups to continue to press for strict scrutiny. Whether this was an effort to create the appearance of reasonableness on her part before the hesitant Court, or acceptance on her part of the need to increase the standard slowly over a greater period of time, is unclear. It could be a combination of both, or conversely, it could indicate an increased faith in the pending ratification of the ERA. It was during this period that Ginsburg traveled extensively speaking to legislatures in the states that had yet to vote on the proposed amendment. For whatever reason, as she indicated to the inquiring *Kahn* note writer, five votes for strict scrutiny was unlikely in 1975, and the main issue to be tackled was which precedent—*Kahn* or *Frontiero*—would be applied to *Weinberger*.

The Supreme Court briefs for both parties in *Weinberger* were predictable, each resembling their arguments in district court, with the addition of their analysis of the applicability of the recently decided *Kahn*. Ginsburg distinguished *Kahn* from *Weinberger*, showing that *Kahn* equalized opportunity for women by remedying past discrimination, while §402(g) denied women opportunity for equal remuneration in the job market. She reasoned that legislatures could both remedy overt discrimination against women, as in *Kahn*, and reject the stereotype in *Weinberger*. She noted that Title VII of the Civil Rights Act of 1964 and the pursuant EEOC Sex Discrimination guidelines made it unlawful for an employer to provide benefits for wives and families not available for husbands and families. She concluded that it would be "bitterly ironic if a differential prohibited by federal command . . . were permitted to stand in federal social insurance."[451] Appellants contended that the governmental interest at stake was not only rationally related to a valid public purpose, but that it could withstand a strict scrutiny challenge. They built on the fact that two of the three *Kahn* dissenters, Brennan and Marshall, agreed that *Kahn* served a compelling interest. Their dissent was based on the broad nature of the Florida statute.[452]

The unanimous decision in *Weinberger*, handed down on March 19, 1975, was an overwhelming success for Ginsburg and vindication of her analysis of *Frontiero*'s far-reaching implications.[453] It represents one of only two decisions where Justice Rehnquist voted to strike down a gender classification in the law—the other was the 1996 VMI case.[454] With Douglas not participating, the remaining eight Justices held that a woman's earnings must garner the same protection for her family that a man's earnings would. They specifically rejected the government's contention that Congress intended to provide an income to women who were unable to provide for themselves because of economic discrimination, as in *Kahn*. Rather, they determined the congressional intent to permit women to elect not to work and devote themselves to raising children, and thus gender-based distinctions that diminished the protection their work afforded them, should they choose to work, could not stand.

FURTHER SOCIAL SECURITY INEQUALITIES

After *Kahn v. Shevin* was handed down by the Court in late 1974, but before the Court had decided *Weinberger v. Wiesenfeld*, the *Kahn* decision made Ginsburg uneasy about the next case, *Coffin v. Secretary of Health, Education, and Welfare*,[455] that was lined up to challenge another inequality in Social Security law. Edgar Coffin was a retired New Jersey policeman who sought the help of the New Jersey chapter of the ACLU to challenge the dependency test for widowers after reading about the filing of Stephen Wiesenfeld's case. His wife, Edna Coffin, had been a math teacher whose earnings were approximately equal to his, although she received a slightly higher pension and was covered by social security while he was not. Coffin's case was nearly identical to Stephan Wiesenfeld minus the dependent child. Both Paula Wiesenfeld and Edna Coffin were denied equal protection because their employment paid out less money—and in Edgar Coffin's situation, no money at all—in survivor's benefits. Ginsburg's strategy was to bring *Coffin* after *Weinberger*, both relying upon the precedent set in the *Frontiero* decision, but the defeat in *Kahn* left her unsure of that path. She had planned to argue that the law denigrates the efforts of wage earning women as demonstrated in *Frontiero*. However, *Kahn* created a strong argument for the government, namely that the law favors widow over widower.[456] To improve her chances for a victory, Ginsburg coordinated with the ACLU state chapters in California, Maryland, New Jersey, Florida, and New York to bring a set of similar cases against the Secretary of Health, Education, and Welfare. However, the progress of the cases once again illustrated the difficulty of orchestrating test case litigation. Although Coffin's case was filed in District Court a full year before the others were initiated in their respective states, *Califano v. Goldfarb*[457] was decided in New York District Court the same week it was argued, three weeks before *Coffin* was handed down. Ginsburg worried over the timing, because, on the merits, *Coffin* was a perfect test case, whereas *Goldfarb* presented the least sympathetic circumstances. Because of Supreme Court procedures, *Goldfarb* was scheduled for oral argument before any of the others.[458]

At the time of argument, Ginsburg described Goldfarb's case as a "cliffhanger," and considered it "*Frontiero* with a heftier price tag," or "*Wiesenfeld* minus the baby."[459] The case originated in Brooklyn, New York with Ginsburg as lead counsel from the time of its arrival in the ACLU office. Along with the other test cases in that set, the challenged social security provision was declared unconstitutional in district court, and *Goldfarb* was argued at the Supreme Court the same day as *Craig v. Boren.*[460]

From oral argument in October until the decision was announced more than four months later, Ginsburg was pessimistic about Goldfarb's chances. Despite the similarity to *Weinberger*, *Goldfarb* had a potential price tag of over $500 million. Also, as Ginsburg wrote to a colleague the day before the decision was announced, "in addition to the money, the Court will no doubt want to discourage the attitude that it is open season on social security classifications."[461] Despite these factors, the "500 million dollar decision" was handed down on March 2, 1977 upholding the lower court ruling, albeit by a slim margin. The same nine Justices that had been unanimous the previous term in *Weinberger* had broken down into a 5-4 split over *Goldfarb*. Justices Brennan, Marshall, White, Powell, and Stevens agreed with the lower court that the dependency provision was unconstitutional. The majority, excepting Stevens, agreed with Ginsburg that the provision was in conflict with their 1975 decision in *Weinberger*, calling the legislation an "archaic and overbroad generalization."[462] In a concurring opinion, Justice Stevens surprised many, including Ginsburg, by picking up on a point by the dissenters, and faulting the provision on the ground that it discriminated against men.[463] In his view, the fact that Social Security benefits are neither contractual nor a compensation for services made Social Security just another tax that could be considered general revenue. He concluded that the provision was "merely the accidental byproduct of a traditional way of thinking about females."[464]

The dissenters, Justices Burger, Blackmun, Rehnquist, and Stewart rejected the contention that the provision was in conflict with the *Weinberger* decision they had joined, depriving Ginsburg of another unanimous victory, and the broad reading of the 1975 decision that she had hoped for. In another ironic turn, *Goldfarb* was announced the day after ERA ratification was defeated in North Carolina. With only two years left before the deadline for ERA ratification, and only a handful of states that looked promising as votes for passage, Ginsburg wrote to Lawrence Wallace, a long term senior member of the Solicitor General's office, "the judgment [in *Goldfarb*] helped cushion the sad news."[465] More uplifting news came the next week as the rest of the test litigation was announced in a series of favorable follow up decisions on March 21, 1977. The Court handed down *Califano v.*

Silbowitz, Califano v. Jablon, and *Califano v. Abbott* together,[466] invalidating the same dependency test at issue in *Goldfarb.*

Although it is often overlooked as a key case in the 1976 term because it was decided without argument and handed down per curiam, *Califano v. Webster*[467] provides crucial information about the state of sex discrimination juxtaposed against the victories in Ginsburg's set of test cases. William Webster brought a case as a pro se litigant challenging the different formulas used to calculate Social Security benefits for women and men. Under Social Security law, retirement benefits were based on an employee's average monthly wage. Before 1972, women who retired were allowed to remove three more low-income years than men when calculating their average earnings over a lifetime of employment. Congress had enacted the law allowing women the more favorable calculation in 1956 in order to provide a small measure of relief to the large percentage of women wage earners who were restricted to the lowest paid positions. In 1972, Congress amended the formula to provide equal treatment for the sexes in the wake of *Reed.* Webster, who turned 65 in 1974, contended he should be able to calculate his earnings on the 15 year basis a woman his age would be able to, instead of the 18 year basis as required by 1974 law. He received a favorable judgment from the New York District Court, despite four other courts around the country who ruled against the litigants in similar suits. The government appealed to the Supreme Court, which considered the case shortly after *Goldfarb* and announced it with the other Social Security cases on March 21, 1977.

In keeping with their view of a very narrow, but acceptable, category of "benign" discrimination in *Kahn,* the Court unanimously decided against Webster.[468] Writing for the majority, Brennan's opinion stressed that discrimination in favor of women was not unconstitutional if it was enacted as a remedy for past discrimination. The Court reasoned that Congress' motives for its 1956 action fit those circumstances.[469] In both *Goldfarb* and *Webster*, the statues at issue were outdated by 1977, but in *Webster's* case, Congress had recognized the violation of equal protection and taken action. The Court deferred to Congress' judgment that the sex neutralization was not retroactive because the 1956 measures were justified by the data on women's status as members of the workforce at that time.

Curious about her reaction to the Court's synthesis of its positions in *Kahn* and *Goldfarb*, one of Brennan's clerks, Jerry Lynch, wrote to Ginsburg two days after the *Webster* announcement. "I drew the assignment of crafting the opinion . . . I attempted to confine legitimate 'benign' discrimination pretty narrowly," he wrote, "throwing in a plug for absolute equality, and yet preserving the possibility that truly compensatory programs can be clearly identified."[470] She replied to Lynch stating, "the *Webster* per curiam shows your fine hand . . . and leaves a corridor for genuine compensation without offering encouragement to lower courts tempted to seize on *Kahn* and *Ballard* whenever confronted with a gender classification."[471]

Ginsburg's comments indicate that she was pleased with the job that the Court had done in adjudicating *Goldfarb* and *Webster*. However, she later chastised the *Goldfarb* dissenters, who concurred together in *Webster*, for failing to see the difference between the two cases. In a short comment sent to various publications outlining the ACLU's position on the outcome of the March cases, she speculated, "with time, and with the aid of the ERA, [perhaps] all of the Justices will come to comprehend the invidiousness of laws . . . rooted in sex discrimination."[472]

She went on in her reply to Lynch to explain that from the time she argued *Goldfarb* until it was handed down, she feared that the Social Security cases in her litigation set might be combined with *Webster*, and the Court, distracted by the potential cost, would decide in favor of the government.[473] The votes in the March 1977 cases, which signaled the dissenters' unwillingness to expand upon *Weinberger*, were no surprise to Ginsburg, although she held mild expectations for Blackmun after his comments about sex discrimination in *Lucas v. Matthews*,[474] a case involving social security benefits payable to the illegitimate child of a deceased parent. Ginsburg reasoned that the dissenters in the four 5-4 cases were willing to give "something to the girls so long as only ad hoc decision making was occurring [in *Weinberger*]. But when those decisions edged toward establishing general principle, they turned back."[475]

The general state of affairs in the struggle for women's equality after March 1977 was muddled. The ERA defeat in North Carolina was disheartening for activists, but focusing solely on ACLU litigation strategy, one could describe the October 1976 term as a banner year for Ginsburg. Three major developments can be identified. First, the early 1970s challenges in *Reed, Frontiero, Kahn, Taylor, Weinberger,* and *Stanton*[476] provided the support for the Court to innovate beyond the rigid two-tiered system of equal protection analysis and announce an intermediate level of review, first in *Craig v. Boren*, then again in *Goldfarb*. Second, although *Goldfarb* did not garner the support *Weinberger* did in sheer number of votes, the plurality opinion did follow *Weinberger* closely enough to make plainly vulnerable scores of laws beyond those concerning survivors' benefits. Following the March decisions, the WRP identified and distributed a list of all the nonconforming statutes state by state, including large numbers of worker compensation and pension schemes, directing all ACLU affiliates to urge legislative revision. Finally, what Ginsburg feared would be the potentially dreadful impact of *Kahn* was halted by implicit clarification made by way of a paired reading of the *Goldfarb* and *Webster* decisions. In sum, legislation that was enacted to remedy past discrimination would be tolerated, so long as it were for an interim period. Otherwise, byproducts of "romantic paternalism" would fall under the new reading of the equal protection clause.[477] Additionally, *Webster* was another example of extension of the offending statute as remedy rather than invalidation.

It is interesting to note Ginsburg's prediction about the effect of precedents set by the sex discrimination cases would have on a case following the 1976 term. Concerning *Regents of the University of California v. Bakke*,[478] Ginsburg delivered the George Abel Dreyfous Lecture towards the end of the 1977 term in which she speculated that the *Webster* decision would provide a "starting point" for the Justices to address Allan Bakke's claim.[479] Indeed, Justices Brennan, White, Marshall, and Blackmun, concurring in part and dissenting in part with the opinion delivered by Justice Powell, quoted from *Kahn* in determining that race, like "gender-based classifications too often [has] been inexcusably utilized to stereotype and stigmatize politically powerless segments of society."[480] They also drew directly from *Webster* at one point in suggesting that compensatory schemes do not automatically pass constitutional muster.[481] Instead, they suggested that the Court take its cue from gender-based discrimination rulings and use the newly sanctioned intermediate tier when adjudicating the merits of racial classifications designed to further remedial purposes. In their words, strict scrutiny in such cases should not be "'strict in theory and fatal in fact' . . . but strict and searching."[482]

Returning to the persistent inequalities in government distributed benefits, Ginsburg continued to hope that the pending ERA would be ratified, but with hope dimming, she persisted in targeting, one by one, state and federal discriminatory laws. In early 1979, with Ginsburg participating as amicus, the Court struck down gender classifications in two separate cases. In *Orr v. Orr*,[483] the Justices divided 8-1 against an Alabama alimony law that awarded benefits based on sex rather than need or ability to pay. In *Califano v. Wescott*,[484] the Court ruled that benefits must be paid to families with unemployed mothers as well as unemployed fathers. In both opinions, Ginsburg was encouraged by the Court's increasing criticism of gratuitous gender-based distinctions. In one of the last cases she participated in as ACLU counsel before being appointed to the federal bench, she assisted the plaintiffs in their challenge to Missouri's workers compensation benefit scheme in *Wengler v. Druggists Mutual Insurance Company*.[485] After *Weinberger*, state supreme courts in the three remaining states, except Missouri, with proof of dependency requirements had invalidated those laws. Ginsburg felt that *Wengler* was "a clear winner, particularly after the unanimous ruling on the constitutional issue in *Westcott*."[486]

Signing onto the case in July 1979, Ginsburg wrote to a colleague "Missouri has done it again!"[487] after receiving word that the Missouri Supreme Court had ruled against Paul Wengler in his request to receive workers compensation death benefits following the death of his wife, Ruth. It was Missouri law that a widower was eligible for such benefits only if he were physically or mentally handicapped or if he depended on his wife for support. Missouri automatically awarded benefits to a widow under a conclusive presumption that she was totally dependent upon her husband's wages for support.[488]

Although Ginsburg found the lead attorney's writing style "abominable," and disagreed with him sharply about the merits of extension over invalidation, she allowed him to take the lead in the case, extending her standard offer of advice and assistance in drafting the appellants brief. In one exchange, she submitted revisions to one of his drafts, indicating that she had "strengthened the psychological impact on the Justices."[489]

She was confident that the Justices would summarily reverse, although she filed as amicus on behalf of the ACLU when they did not.

As expected, Missouri's law was ruled unconstitutional in an 8-1 decision handed down in April 1980, with Rehnquist dissenting. In his dissent, Rehnquist wrote that *Goldfarb* had been wrongly decided and that constitutional issues should be examined more closely under *stare decisis* than other decisions.[490] In a comical summary of the dissent, the *New*

York Times reported, "Justice Rehnquist dissented on the ground that he continue[s] to regard all the Court's recent decisions in this area as wrong."[491] Writing for the majority, Justice White declared that gender-based classifications must serve important governmental objectives,[492] which Ginsburg praised as another clear enunciation of heightened scrutiny, with the burden of proof being shifted to the defender of discrimination. Writing to her research assistant, she stated, "it was unrealistic to expect the Court to embrace our suspect classification argument—but we can still be thankful for small things."[493]

CRAIG V. BOREN: SIX SOLID VOTES FOR A MIDDLE TIER

In Ginsburg's view, the 1976 term represented a transition into the third phase of her litigation strategy, bringing with it new opportunities and new constraints. Looking back, she categorized the period from 1971-1973 as a revived women's movement signaled by the Equal Pay Act, Title VII, and the beginning of the hard push for an Equal Rights Amendment which complimented the victories in *Reed, Stanley,* and *Frontiero.* The second phase was marked by line holding, or in some cases, retrenchment, represented by *Kahn, Geduldig,*[495] and *LaFleur.*[496] Although a case like *Kahn* might eventually have been incorporated into Ginsburg's strategy, she spoke openly about her frustration that it came out of turn and considered it a pitfall.[497] Despite the bad timing of *Kahn,* history indicates that the Court was not unduly influenced by its proximity to *DeFunis*[498] as Ginsburg suspected. Later in 1974, the Court refused once more to declare "benign favors" discriminatory when in *Geduldig* it upheld a California statute excluding pregnancy as a disability claim under a worker's income protection disability insurance plan.

October term 1975 brought the Court back to the *Reed* and *Frontiero* track. *Taylor v. Louisiana*[499] overturned *Hoyt,* preempting Ginsburg's efforts to do just that with *Edwards v.*

Healy,[500] although the eventual outcome was in keeping with the mission of the Women's Rights Project. In addition, she was handed her first victory against Social Security differentials in *Weinberger*, a victory she felt set the record straight after the fallout in *Kahn*.

Preparing for the third phase of her strategy, Ginsburg's personal notes and outlines indicate her awareness of the mindset of the Court and her intention to incorporate their "perception problem" into her arguments. In addition, she continued to be mindful that a majority of the Justices held tight to the original intention of the Fourteenth Amendment with race as its core concern. In light of what she referred to as this "historic drag,"[501] she decided to abandon her strict scrutiny argument for the time, noting in one outline that there was "a danger in arguing suspect post-*Aiello*."[502] By early 1976 she had come to view the key to understanding the Court's decisions from *Reed* to the present in terms of process instead of product. She recognized that the Court had shied away from exactly what she argued for—doctrinal development. Instead, the Court donned blinders, deciding each case as an isolated set of circumstances while she was attempting to expose systematic, widespread discrimination. The Court's belief that applying the Fourteenth Amendment to gender discrimination represented a considerable stretch in the intentions of the Founding Fathers and the Reconstruction Congress allowed Ginsburg to revamp her strategy to accommodate less than the strict scrutiny goal that had occupied her arguments since 1971.

In public appearances, Ginsburg was often called upon to comment on the refusal of the Court to decided cases squarely on the equal protection clause. In one particular speech to the League of Women voters in 1976, she rhetorically asked, "If the government shall not deny to any person the equal protection of the laws, can't equal rights advocates use that handle to challenge discriminatory laws in court, and through that means, impel legislative change?"[503] She answered that the problem was that equal protection came with a history. She explained that the Reconstruction Congress had absolutely no intention to target gender-based discrimination. In her words, "Why should they? When the 13th, 14th, and 15th Amendments were added to the Constitution, women could not vote, contract, hold property, or even litigate on their own behalf."[504]

She took to heart Justice Powell's 1975 expression of the Court's consideration of its own position as a governmental branch. He publicly acknowledged that the Court must act with particular circumspection in the dim zone between constitutional interpretation and constitutional amendment. Furthermore, he said that the Court should not move boldly under equal protection at the very time when state legislatures, functioning within the traditional democratic process, are debating the ERA.[505] Ginsburg went so far as to praise the Justices' publicly for the steps they had taken. In an August 30, 1976 newspaper article, she was quoted as saying, "from the viewpoint of feminists, the Burger Court has been far superior to other courts."[506] Ever the strategist, she viewed the October 1976 term as an opportunity to seek what the Justices seemed willing to give—a solid ruling imposing a new test of state gender classifications, something less than the strict scrutiny accorded racial distinctions, but more than the rational relation test with which *Reed* and *Frontiero* had been decided.

During the summer of 1975, Ginsburg attempted to convince the Court to decide *Edwards* on its merits and not to moot the case as Louisiana's counsel had requested. In writing the briefs for the case, she began corresponding with Fred Gilbert, an Oklahoma attorney who was representing Curtis Craig in an equal protection challenge. Although the two cases were circumstantially very different, in Craig's case, Oklahoma had based the statute in question upon scientific evidence about the differing mental processes of men and women. Researching for the *Edwards* brief, Ginsburg discovered that counsel for Gwendolyn Hoyt made a similar argument in that 1961 case. She and Gilbert began sharing their research, and she became interested in incorporating his case, *Craig v. Boren*, into her larger litigation strategy should it reach the Supreme Court. Prior to 1971, Oklahoma defined the age of majority to be age 18 for females and age 21 for males, despite their decision that females could be held criminally responsible at age 18 and males at age 16. Following *Reed v. Reed*, the Tenth Circuit Court of Appeals held that the age distinction was no longer constitutional and fixed the universal age of criminal responsibility for adults at 18. This age requirement was also applied to individuals in civil matters except for 15 Oklahoma Statute §§241 and 245 concerning the purchase of 3.2% beer, mandating that women were legally allowed to buy "near beer" at age 18, whereas males were restricted until age 21.[507] Petitioners Carolyn Whitener, proprietor of the Honk and Holler convenience store, and Curtis Craig, her would-be customer, brought the challenge. They lost in the Tenth Circuit in May 1975, and they appealed to the Supreme Court.[508]

Writing to Ginsburg in November of that year, Gilbert invited the ACLU to appear as amicus after the Court noted probable jurisdiction in the case. In contrast to the hard line attitude Ginsburg took with Joseph Levin in *Frontiero* concerning argument before the Supreme Court, Ginsburg wrote to Gilbert accepting his offer, noting, "my participation in the oral argument is not a condition [of acceptance]. In view of your long, hard efforts in this case, the day in court certainly belongs to you if you want it."[509] She did, however, attempt to convince Gilbert that she should write his brief, although she indicated a willingness to file as amicus if he declined.[510] Gilbert did politely decline her offer to author the appellants' brief, stating only that collaboration would be too complicated given their geographic distance.[511] Ginsburg agreed with his point, but nonetheless continued to read his drafts and revise accordingly in a thinly veiled attempt to tailor the case to her litigation strategy. Gilbert was enormously grateful for her assistance. In fact, it was at Ginsburg's suggestion that Gilbert compared the discrimination in *Craig* with the Michigan law upheld in *Goesaert*. Of the four cases that the WRP has identified as targets to overturn, *Goesaert* was the only outstanding case by late 1975. Ginsburg stated that "protecting the boys against the 3.2 beer parlors contrast[ed] nicely."[512]

Many scholars have speculated about the absence of an argument for strict scrutiny in *Craig* comparable to that in Ginsburg's *Reed* and *Frontiero* challenges. Indeed, without the benefit of her personal notes and correspondence with Gilbert, it seems odd that Ginsburg, with a litigation strategy that had achieved such gains in such a short period of time, would abandon the ultimate goal. As previously noted, the key lies in Ginsburg's increasing political acumen. Having become adept at arguing to the nine men on the Court, rather than fighting on general principle, she urged Gilbert to take a similar tack. "We don't have five votes for suspect classification, so play that down," she wrote, "urge instead heightened scrutiny as evidenced in Reed, Frontiero, Wiesenfeld, and Stanton."[513]

Throughout February 1976, Ginsburg continued her attempt to convert her amicus brief to the appellants brief. She sent Gilbert installments of her work as they were completed and advised him on his efforts, stating that she "remain[ed] of the strong view that one brief is the better way."[514] As late as February 20, 1976, she informed the printer to leave out the page numbers when type setting her brief to avoid unnecessary complications should Gilbert acquiesce and agree to submit her brief as the appellants' argument.[515] In the end, Ginsburg did file as amicus, although her impact on the appellants' brief cannot be overstated. A week before the filing, the Court noted probable jurisdiction in *Goldfarb*, the second of Ginsburg's challenges to Social Security differentials after *Weinberger*. Before filing, Gilbert sent her the final copy of the appellants brief, noting that he had "succeeded in excising everything that could have been prejudicial to your other litigation."[516] Although she regarded the "beer case" as "something of an embarrassment,"[517] she recognized that its outcome could be significant for *Goldfarb*, and kept close tabs on Gilbert's progress, fearing another situation like the unfortunate pairing of *DeFunis* and *Kahn*.

Preempting Gilbert's efforts to author the reply to Oklahoma's brief, Ginsburg sent him her "idea of an appropriate reply."[518] Gilbert adopted her brief and suggested some minor changes, the majority of which she talked him out of. One change in particular involved the question of whether or not to urge the square overruling of *Goesaert*. It was Ginsburg who initially suggested the inclusion of *Goesaert* in his original submission, but as for extending the argument, she convinced him to leave well enough alone. Indicative of her increased seasoning as a politician, as well as an advocate before the Court, she declined to continue the attack on Frankfurter she began in *Frontiero*. Instead, she counseled Gilbert to use *Moose Lodge*,[519] which presented an "exhaustive treatment of the 21st Amendment." She reasoned that it was "better to give the Court its own recent precedent as a peg than beat harder on Frankfurter for his blind spot."[520] She continued to approve, or disapprove of, Gilbert's stylistic changes to the reply brief throughout the summer of 1976, and agreed to sit at the counsel table with him during oral argument—made easier by the serendipitous scheduling of *Goldfarb* and *Craig* for the same day. In fact, Ginsburg had her staff arrange with the Clerk of the Court, Michael Rodak, that *Goldfarb* follow *Craig* so that Ginsburg could "keep friend Fred on a straight and narrow path."[521]

Despite her intention, Ginsburg was unable to keep Gilbert from what amounted to a poor showing in his appearance before the Court. Already embarrassed that the "ridiculous" Oklahoma law had received so much national attention, she must have been mortified by Gilbert's sarcastic commentary on the motives of the state legislature, which included, "the purpose behind the law is to allow young women to drown their sorrows in 3.2 beer."[522] He went on to dispute the state's argument that the law was passed to reduce the number of drunken teenage drivers, noting that "it is possible to get drunk on 3.2 beer, but you have to force it down to do so."[523] At one point, his rhetoric was so extreme that Chief Justice Burger warned him about exaggerating.[524]

Despite Gilbert's antics, the challenge in *Craig* was successful. In 1948, Justice Frankfurter wrote in *Goesaert* concerning the Michigan ban on women as bartenders that "to ask whether [such a law violated the Fourteenth Amendment's equal protection clause was] in effect to answer it."[525] Precisely 28 years to the day later, the Court did answer that question in *Craig*. Writing for six Justices, Justice Brennan disposed of *Goesaert* in a three-sentence footnote in an opinion holding that "classifications by gender must serve important governmental objectives and must be substantially related to achievement of those objectives."[526] Chief Justice Burger advised Brennan when assigning the opinion that he would join if it were narrowly written, but following the second draft, Burger sent a terse memorandum to Brennan stating, "you have read into *Reed v. Reed* what is not there. Every gender distinction does not need the strict scrutiny test applicable to a criminal case. *Reed* was the innocuous matter of who was to probate an estate. As written, I cannot possibly join."[527] Although Ginsburg would disagree with Burger's assessment of *Reed*, it was no matter, the battle at hand had been won. Newspapers across the country featured editorials not only praising the Court for its decision in *Craig*, but also calling for the elevation of gender to the level of scrutiny accorded race.[528]

Chapter VI
Looking Back, Looking Ahead

Toward the end of her career as head of the ACLU Women's Rights Project, many of Ruth Bader Ginsburg's colleagues expressed optimism that she would soon be appointed the federal bench. After a decade as a lawyer and advocate for equality, Ginsburg had received widespread recognition as the architect of the litigation strategy that effected a profound change not only in the law, but also in the mindset of many leading jurists, including the Justices of the United States Supreme Court. Thus, it came as no surprise that President Jimmy Carter appointed Ginsburg to the U.S. Court of Appeals for the District of Columbia Circuit—a stepping stone to the high Court.

Reflecting in 1979 on the success of the movement to develop equity in the law for men and women, Ginsburg was optimistic about the future and content with the developments throughout the 1970s. Although many observers were disheartened by the Court's unwillingness to elevate gender to the level of a suspect class after a decade of challenges, Ginsburg had more reasonable expectations, and felt that "those depressed hoped for too much too soon."[529] She believed that her optimistic outlook arose from her age, her ability to recognize institutional limitations on the courts, and her continued focus on the social and economic trends in society that would exert pressure on lawmakers.

In all of the briefs she composed on equal protection issues, observers will see her argument for judging gender-based classifications by a higher standard than the rational relation test because gender is an inalienable trait, and in many she directly links the logic behind discrimination based on gender to that of race. However, she did not think that the Burger Court had failed women where the Warren Court supplied justice to racial minorities. In fact, she often stated publicly that from a feminist standpoint, the Burger Court was far superior to its predecessors. Rather, she recognized that the Supreme Court was able to move farther and faster in elevating race to the level of a suspect class because history and society made it possible. In essence, Thurgood Marshall and the NAACP had a foundation to build on that Ginsburg and the Women's Rights Project did not. Because the Reconstruction Congress had amended the Constitution with racial concerns at the core of their concern, the Warren Court was able to advance rapidly in that area, although they exposed themselves to concerns of legislating change even with this historical backing. Knowing this history was the prime motivation for Ginsburg to expend substantial time and energy attempting to convince states to ratify the Equal Rights Amendment. Failing to accomplish this, she knew that limitations on the Court were present, and only more time and space for reflection would impel the federal judiciary to advance.

Few doubt the impact that Ginsburg had on advancing the needs of women and their families in the law. What is equally apparent is that it impacted her, both personally and professionally, as well. In the early 1970s, her faith ran high that the Justices would take her briefs to heart and begin to adjudicate gender-based classifications for what they were— rarely benign and generally rigid sex stereotyping that was antiquated and harmful. After *Frontiero* was decided in 1973, the prospect for a majority of the Court to embrace Ginsburg's position was bright. Although it may be seen as a retreat on Brennan's part to temper his *Frontiero* position and write for the majority instead of a plurality in later cases, Ginsburg would disagree. She recognized, as a seasoned political observer, that had Justice Brennan not done so, there would not have been a majority opinion in such crucial decisions as *Weinberger*, *Craig*, and *Orr*. What some have observed as abandonment of her ultimate goal in the later years is actually an astute calculation on her part. Her decision not to press strict scrutiny in the same manner as she did in the early 1970s was a crucial factor in securing the application of intermediate scrutiny, which has now lasted for over 25 years, and was necessary groundwork for decisions like the Virginia Military Institute opinion—appropriately written by now Justice Ginsburg.

Since 1996, states have been put on notice that they must provide an "exceedingly persuasive justification" for laws that discriminate on the basis of gender. Court watchers and scholarly observers greeted such justification with the implicit assumption that it carried with it the realization of Ginsburg's mission, effectively enacting the ERA. Following the VMI opinion, Ginsburg said of the possibility of a revived movement to enact an Equal Rights Amendment "there is no practical difference between what has evolved and the ERA."[530] More recently, commenting on a June 2001 decision, she wrote, "sadly no . . . there is the aberrational *Ngyuen*."[531] In *Ngyuen*, the Court was asked to decide whether citizenship rules for children born abroad and out of wedlock depending on whether the citizen parent is the mother or the father were consistent with the equal protection guarantee embedded in the Fifth Amendments Due Process Clause. In a 5-4 decision with Ginsburg dissenting, the Court decided that the statute was constitutional.[532]

Asked about her own contributions, she would modestly attribute the advancements in the law to the Burger Court. Perhaps the best indication of her success can be found in the evaluations of her career, not by her supporters, but by those who opposed the ERA when it was under consideration, and similarly have opposed Ginsburg's advancement of its judicial equivalent on the bench under the Equal Protection Clause of the Fourteenth Amendment. The Independent Women's Forum, a group that is far less independent than its name would suggest, published an article in its own magazine in 1997 stating "the ERA has quietly and stealthily become the law of the land thanks to 25 years of Supreme Court decisions, first guided and then written by ERA advocate and now Justice Ruth Bader Ginsburg."[533] For Justice Ginsburg, there is no truer statement and no higher praise.

Chronology

March 15, 1933   Ruth Bader Ginsburg born in Brooklyn, New York

1954   Received B.A., Cornell University
Married Martin Ginsburg

1956-1958   Attended Harvard Law School

1959   Received L.L.B., Columbia University School of Law

1959-1961   Law clerk to Judge Edmund L. Palmieri, United States District Court, Southern District, New York

1961-1962   Research Associate, Columbia University School of Law

1962-1963   Associate Director of project on international procedure, Columbia University School of Law

1963-1972   Professor, Rutgers Law School, Newark, New Jersey
1963-1966, Assistant Professor
1966-1969, Associate Professor
1969-1972, Professor

1965   Published with Anders Bruzelius, *Civil Procedure in Sweden*

1968   Edited with Anders Bruzelius, *Swedish Code of Judicial Procedure*

1971   Visiting Professor, Harvard Law School

1972-1973   Founder and Director, ACLU Women's Rights Project

1973-1980   General Counsel, ACLU

1972-1980   Professor, Columbia University School of Law

1974   Published with Kenneth Davidson and Herma Hill Kay, *Text, Cases, and Materials on Sex-Based Discrimination*

1977-1978   Fellow, Center for Advanced Study in Behavioral Sciences, Stanford, California

1980-1993   Judge, U. S. Court of Appeals for the District of Columbia Circuit

1993-   Associate Justice of the United States Supreme Court

TIMELINE OF MAJOR SUPREME COURT DECISIONS ON WOMEN'S RIGHTS

PREPARED BY THE ACLU WOMEN'S RIGHTS PROJECT, MAY 2003

1971

Reed v. Reed, 404 U.S. 71 (1971). In this case, the United States Supreme Court rules for the first time ever that a law that discriminates against women is unconstitutional under the Fourteenth Amendment. In reaching this result, the Court relies on a brief written by Professor Ruth Bader Ginsburg, the ACLU Women's Rights Project's first director. The Court rules unanimously that a state statute that provides that males must be preferred to females in estate administration denies women equal protection of the law.

Phillips v. Martin Marietta, 400 U.S. 542 (1971). The Supreme Court rules that an employer violates Title VII when it refuses to hire women with young children while hiring men who are similarly situated.

1973

Frontiero v. Richardson, 411 U.S. 677 (1973). In this case, initially filed by the Southern Poverty Law Center, and the first argued before the Supreme Court by Professor Ginsburg, the Court strikes down a federal statute that automatically grants male members of the uniformed forces housing and benefits for their wives, but requires female members to demonstrate the "actual dependency" of their husbands to qualify for the same benefit. Four Justices conclude that laws differentiating by sex are inherently suspect and subject to strict judicial scrutiny, as are those differentiating by race.

Pittsburgh Press v. Pittsburgh Commission on Human Relations, 413 U.S. 376 (1973). The Supreme Court holds that employers' use of sex-segregated "Male Help Wanted" and "Female Help Wanted" columns and newspapers' publication of these columns is illegal, because sex-segregated columns enable employers to express unlawful gender preferences. On behalf of the Women's Rights Project, Professor Ginsburg co-authors an amicus brief in the case.

1974

Geduldig v. Aiello, 417 U.S. 484 (1974). On behalf of the Women's Rights Project, Professor Ginsburg co-authors an amicus brief that argues that laws discriminating on the basis of pregnancy make gender-based distinctions and should be evaluated under heightened scrutiny. The Court holds that a disability insurance program that denies benefits for disabilities resulting from pregnancy is not unconstitutional, as it does not involve discrimination on the basis of gender, but discrimination between pregnant and non-pregnant persons.

Kahn v. Shevin, 416 U.S. 351 (1974). In this Women's Rights Project case, originally filed by the ACLU of Florida, the Court holds that a Florida statute granting widows, but not widowers, an annual five hundred dollar exemption from property taxes is constitutional because the purpose of the statute is to close the gap between men and women's economic situations and there is a substantial relationship between this purpose and the exemption.

Corning Glass Works v. Brennan, 417 U.S. 188 (1974). The Supreme Court for the first time considers an Equal Pay Act claim based on an employer paying women less than men for the same work. It determines that the wage difference between Corning's female day inspectors and male night inspectors violates the Equal Pay Act. Professor Ginsburg, on behalf of the Women's Rights Project, authors an amicus brief.

1975

Weinberger v. Weisenfeld, 420 U.S. 636 (1975). Professor Ginsburg, on behalf of the Women's Rights Project, successfully argues that a provision of the Social Security Act providing for gender-based distinctions in the award of social security benefits is unconstitutional. In this case, the Court holds that the government cannot provide child-in-care benefits to widows with minor children and not to widowers, since such a provision discriminates against working women, whose families receive fewer protections as a result of their social security taxes than do men, and against widowers, who need such benefits in order to devote themselves to their children.

Cleveland Board of Education v. LaFleur, 414 U.S. 632 (1975). The Supreme Court holds that it is unconstitutional for public employers to require women to take unpaid maternity leaves after the first trimester of pregnancy because of a conclusive presumption that pregnant women are no longer able to work, since such policies impinge on women's due process rights.

On behalf of the Women's Rights Project, Professor Ginsburg co-authors an amicus brief in the case.

Taylor v. Louisiana, 419 U.S. 522 (1975). The Supreme Court invalidates a Louisiana statute that allows women to serve as jurors only when they expressly volunteer, which has the practical effect of almost entirely eliminating women from juries, and requires states to call men and women to jury service on an equal basis.

Stanton v. Stanton, 421 U.S. 7 (1975). The Supreme Court rules that a law setting the age of majority for women at eighteen and for men at twenty-one, based on the assumption that women need less education and preparation for adulthood than do men, is unconstitutional.

Turner v. Department of Employment Security, 423 U.S. 44 (1975). In this Women's Rights Project case, the Supreme Court invalidates a state regulation making pregnant women ineligible for unemployment benefits for twelve weeks before birth and six weeks after birth regardless of their capacity to work.

1976

Craig v. Boren, 429 U.S. 190 (1976). The Supreme Court adopts a "heightened scrutiny" standard of review to evaluate legal distinctions on the basis of gender, which requires that a gender-based legal distinction bear a substantial relationship to an important governmental interest. This conclusion is based in part on a Women's Rights Project amicus brief written by Professor Ginsburg. The Women's Rights Project works closely with the plaintiffs' attorney in the case.

Regents of the University of California v. Bakke, 429 U.S. 953 (1976). On behalf of the Women's Rights Project, Professor

Ginsburg co-authors an amicus brief to the Court successfully defending affirmative action in public higher education.

General Electric Co. v. Gilbert, 429 U.S.125 (1976). Professor Ginsburg, on behalf of the Women's Rights Project, authors an amicus brief to the Court, arguing that the exclusion of pregnancy-related conditions from a private employer's disability plan violates Title VII. The Court again concludes that pregnancy-based discrimination is not sex discrimination. Congress will override this decision in 1978, through passage of the Pregnancy Discrimination Act.

1977

Califano v. Goldfarb, 430 U.S. 199 (1977). In this Women's Rights Project case, argued by Professor Ginsburg, the Supreme Court invalidates gender-based distinctions in the payment of social security survivor benefits, finding these distinctions to be based on archaic assumptions regarding women's dependency.

Dothard v. Rawlinson, 433 U.S. 321 (1977). The Supreme Court invalidates Alabama's height and weight requirements for prison guards that have the effect of excluding the vast majority of female candidates, finding that these requirements violate Title VII. However, the Court upholds Alabama's exclusion of women from many jobs as prison guards in all-male maximum security prisons, finding that in such an environment, women could present a security risk. Professor Ginsburg, on behalf of the Women's Rights Project, co-authors an amicus brief in the case.

Coker v. Georgia, 433 U.S. 584 (1977). The Supreme Court holds that Georgia's statute allowing a sentence of death for a convicted rapist is cruel and unusual punishment in violation of the Eighth Amendment. On behalf of the Women's Rights

Project, Professor Ginsburg co-authors an amicus brief opposing the imposition of the death penalty on a convicted rapist because historically, convicted rapists were sentenced to death as a result of the idea that a woman was a man's property and because the severity of such a sentence meant that often police would refuse to charge men with rape and juries would refuse to convict men of rape.

Nashville Gas Co. v. Satty, 434 U.S. 136 (1977). The Court finds that an employer's policy of denying accumulated seniority to employees returning from pregnancy leave violates Title VII in the absence of proof of business necessity of such a practice. The Women's Rights Project co-authors an amicus brief.

1978

Los Angeles Department of Water and Power v. Manhart, 435 U.S. 702 (1978). On behalf of the Women's Rights Project, Professor Ginsburg co-authors an amicus brief for this case in which the Supreme Court holds that requiring female workers to make larger pension fund contributions than their male counterparts violates Title VII since Title VII prevents employers from basing personnel policies on assumptions about differences between men and women as groups.

1979

Duren v. Missouri, 439 U.S. 357 (1979). On behalf of the Women's Rights Project, Professor Ginsburg successfully argues to the Supreme Court that a state statute exempting women from jury duty upon their request violates a defendant's Sixth and Fourteenth Amendment rights to be tried by a jury drawn from a fair cross-section of the community.

Orr v. Orr, 440 U.S. 268 (1979). On behalf of the Women's Rights Project, Professor Ginsburg authors an amicus brief for this case, in which the Supreme Court invalidates statutes providing that husbands, but not wives, may be required to pay alimony upon divorce and thus casts off the assumption that wives are dependent upon their husbands for financial support but husbands are never dependent on wives.

Califano v. Westcott, 443 U.S. 76 (1979). On behalf of the Women's Rights Project, Professor Ginsburg authors an amicus brief that helps persuade the Supreme Court to invalidate a program for unemployment benefits under the Aid to Families with Dependent Children program. The program provides benefits to families with unemployed fathers, but not to those with unemployed mothers, and the Court rules it is therefore unconstitutional because of its presumption that fathers are primary breadwinners while mothers' employment is secondary.

Personnel Administrator of Massachusetts v. Feeney, 442 U.S. 256 (1979). In a challenge to legislation that unquestionably burdens women disproportionately to men by providing a lifetime employment preference for state government jobs to veterans, who are overwhelmingly male, the Court concludes that such a preference is not unconstitutional, since it was adopted "in spite of" rather than "because of" its harmful effect on women.

1980

Wengler v. Druggists Mutual Insurance Co., 446 U.S. 142 (1980). The Court strikes down a state law denying widowers' worker's compensation benefits upon the work-related death of their wives unless they prove dependency or incapacity, while granting widows such benefits automatically. Professor Ginsburg, on behalf of the Women's Rights Project, co-authors an amicus brief in the case.

1981

Kirchberg v. Feenstra, 450 U.S. 455 (1981). This Supreme Court case is the first to invalidate a law that gives a husband the right to control marital property without his wife's consent. Feenstra's husband signed a promissory note mortgaging their marital home to his attorney without telling his wife, pursuant to a Louisiana statute that gave husbands the exclusive right to dispose of community property. The Supreme Court overturns the Louisiana law as an abridgement of married women's constitutional rights under the Equal Protection Clause of the Fourteenth Amendment.

County of Washington v. Gunther, 452 U.S. 161 (1981). In this case, in which the Women's Rights Project submits a key amicus brief, the Court holds that individuals can show illegal gender-based wage discrimination under Title VII even when no member of the opposite sex holds a nearly identical job. This case is important for combating wage discrimination, given continued patterns of gender segregation in employment.

Rostker v. Goldberg, 523 U.S. 57 (1981). The Supreme Court holds that mandatory draft registration for men only does not violate the Constitution. In this case, in which the Women's Rights Project serves as co-counsel for plaintiffs challenging the gender-based requirement, the Court holds that in questions of military service, special deference is accorded to Congress to make such gender-based distinctions.

1982

Mississippi University for Women v. Hogan, 458 U.S. 718 (1982). The Supreme Court rules that it is unconstitutional for a state to provide a nursing school for women only, since there is no important governmental interest in perpetuating women's over-representation in the nursing field.

1983

Arizona Governing Committee v. Norris, 463 U.S. 1073 (1983). The Court holds that a state pension plan that allows employees to choose retirement benefits from one of several companies, all of which pay women lower benefits than men, violates Title VII. The Women's Rights Project authors an amicus brief.

Newport News Shipbuilding & Dry Dock Co. v. EEOC, 462 U.S. 669 (1983). In this case the Supreme Court acknowledges that the Pregnancy Discrimination Act establishes that discrimination based on a woman's pregnancy is, on its face, discrimination because of sex, and thus supercedes Gilbert. The case is brought by male employees who claim that the employer's health plan, which covered pregnancy-related services for female employees more fully than for spouses of male employees, discriminates on the basis of sex. The Court holds that such differentiation is indeed discrimination forbidden under Title VII.

1984

Roberts v. United States Jaycees, 468 U.S. 609 (1984). The Women's Rights Project co-authors an amicus brief in this case, urging the Supreme Court to affirm the state decision to strike down the Jaycees' policy of excluding women under state public accommodations law. The Court does so, holding that the Jaycees's exclusionary practices are not protected by the First Amendment and that Minnesota has a compelling interest in ending sex discrimination.

Hishon v. King & Spalding, 467 U.S. 69 (1984). The Supreme Court finds that partnerships, such as the respondent Atlanta law firm, are "employers" subject to Title VII's prohibition against sex discrimination, and that Title VII requires the law firm to consider women for partnership. The Women's Rights Project co-authors an amicus brief in this case.

1986

Meritor Savings Bank v. Vinson, 477 U.S. 57 (1986). The Supreme Court holds that sexual harassment that creates a hostile environment is a form of sex discrimination prohibited by Title VII.

1987

California Federal Savings & Loan Association v. Guerra 479 U.S. 272 (1987). In this case, an employer seeks a declaration that a state law requiring employers to provide pregnancy leave and reinstatement is preempted by the Pregnancy Discrimination Act's requirement that pregnancy be treated like other disabilities. The Court holds that the Pregnancy Discrimination Act does not prohibit practices favoring pregnant women, and in any case, employers are free to provide comparable benefits to other disabled employees. The Women's Rights Project files an amicus brief.

Wimberly v. Labor & Industrial Relations Commission, 479 U.S. 511 (1987). The Supreme Court holds that a Missouri statute denying unemployment benefits to claimants who leave work "voluntarily" and "without good cause" attributable to work or to the employer can be applied to workers who leave because of pregnancy and is not preempted by a federal law that provides that no state can deny unemployment benefits to an individual solely on the basis of pregnancy. The ACLU Women's Rights Project filed an amicus brief.

Johnson v. Transportation Agency, Santa Clara, 480 U.S. 616 (1987). In this Title VII case brought by a male employee who was passed over for promotion in favor of a female employee with a lower test score, the Supreme Court holds that an employer can take sex into account in such situations if it does so pursuant to an affirmative action plan meant to remedy the under-representation of women in traditionally sex-segregated jobs.

1989

Price-Waterhouse v. Hopkins, 490 U.S. 228 (1989). In this Title VII case, the Supreme Court holds that when gender discrimination plays a part in an employer's decision about an employee, an employer may still avoid Title VII liability if it proves that other reasons played a large enough role in the decision that it would have made the same decision in the absence of discrimination. The Women's Rights Project co-authors a major amicus brief in the case. The Hopkins holding will be partially amended by Congress in the Civil Rights Act of 1991, which provides that an employee proves a violation of Title VII when she shows that discrimination plays any part in an employment decision, but may only receive damages if the employer fails to show that it would have made the same decision even in the absence of discrimination.

1990

Yellow Freight System, Inc. v. Donnelly, 494 U.S. 820 (1990). The Supreme Court holds that state courts, as well as federal courts, can hear Title VII claims. The case involves a woman who sought employment as a dock worker and was repeatedly passed over in favor of male candidates, though the company had assured her that it would hire her as soon as a position became available.

University of Pennsylvania v. EEOC, 493 U.S. 182 (1990). This case involves a claim by a Wharton Business School professor who was denied tenure that the reason for the denial was the negative evaluation of a department chairman who had sexually harassed her; the professor denied tenure argues that her qualifications were equal to or better than the five male professors who were granted tenure. The Supreme Court holds that universities have no common law or First Amendment privilege to withhold peer review materials relevant to charges of race or sexual discrimination in tenure decisions.

1991

United Auto Workers v. Johnson Controls, 499 U.S. 187 (1991). The Women's Rights Project authors an amicus brief that helps persuade the Supreme Court that Title VII forbids employers from adopting fetal-protection policies preventing fertile women from working in jobs that entail exposure to lead or other toxins that might harm a fetus. The case holds that women must be allowed to make their own decisions about pregnancy and dangerous work, and as long as women can perform their jobs, employers may not exclude them from certain kinds of work based on expressions of concern for children they might conceive.

1992

Franklin v. Gwinnet County Public Schools, 503 U.S. 60 (1992). The Supreme Court holds that Title IX supports a claim for monetary damages. In this case the high school student seeking damages claims she was sexually harassed and abused by her teacher and coach and that administrators were aware of the harassment and abuse but took no action to stop it and encouraged her not to press charges against the teacher.

1993

Harris v. Forklift Systems, 510 U.S. 17 (1993). The Supreme Court holds that a person does not have to prove psychological damage in order to prevail in a sexual harassment suit, but can win based on evidence of conduct that would reasonably be perceived to be hostile and sexually abusive.

1996

United States v. Virginia, 518 U.S. 515 (1996). Justice Ginsburg delivers the opinion of the court, ruling that the all-male Virginia Military Institute's (VMI) discriminatory admissions policy violates women's equal protection rights and ordering the school to admit women or forfeit its government funding. The Women's Rights Project participates in this case as amicus and as advisor.

M.L.B v. S.L.J., 519 U.S. 102 (1996). The Supreme Court holds that a state may not deny a parent the right to appeal termination of parental rights because poverty prevents her paying for the record; the state must supply the record itself.

1998

Oncale v. Sundowner Offshore Services, 523 U.S. 75 (1998). The Supreme Court unanimously holds that Title VII prohibits same-sex sexual harassment. The case involves a male offshore oil rig worker who was subjected to sex-related humiliating actions by male co-workers and physically assaulted in a sexual manner by two male co-workers and a supervisor. The Women's Rights Project co-authors an amicus brief in the case.

Faragher v. City of Boca Raton, 524 U.S. 775 (1998). The Supreme Court holds that when a harassing supervisor with authority over an employee takes a "tangible employment action" against the employee, the employer is strictly liable for the supervisor's action under Title VII. The Women's Rights Project co-authors an amicus brief in the case.

Burlington Industries v. Ellerth, 524 U.S. 742 (1998). In this sexual harassment case, a companion to Faragher, the Court again holds that an employer is automatically subject to vicarious liability for an actionable hostile environment created by a supervisor when tangible employment action is taken. If no such "tangible employment action" has taken place, the employer may claim that it exercised reasonable care to prevent and correct promptly any sexually harassing behavior and that the plaintiff employee unreasonably failed to take advantage of any preventive or corrective opportunities provided by the employer.

Gebser v. Lago Vista Independent School District, 524 U.S. 274 (1998). The Supreme Court makes clear the circumstances under which schools are liable for damages when a teacher sexually harasses a student. The Court holds that under Title IX, a school is liable for damages when a school official with knowledge of the teacher's harassment and authority to take corrective action acts with "deliberate indifference" to the teacher's conduct.

1999

Saenz v. Roe, 526 U.S. 489 (1999). The Supreme Court holds that California's one-year residency requirement for individuals seeking full welfare benefits is an unconstitutional violation of individuals' right to travel, as protected by the Fourteenth Amendment.

Davis v. Monroe County Board of Education, 526 U.S. 629 (1999). The Supreme Court rules that school districts may be liable under Title IX for student-to-student harassment if they are aware of the problem and act with "deliberate indifference" rather than try to resolve it. The Women's Rights Project participates as an amicus.

Miller v. Albright, 523 U.S. 420 (1999). The Supreme Court upholds different rules for unmarried citizen fathers versus those for unmarried citizen mothers who wish to transmit citizenship to their foreign-born, out-of-wedlock children. The Women's Rights Project co-authors an amicus brief in the case.

Kolstad v. American Dental Association, 527 U.S. 526 (1999). In this sex discrimination case, the Supreme Court holds that a court may grant punitive damages to a woman alleging sex discrimination in violation of Title VII even if she does not show that the employer's conduct was "egregious" or "outrageous." Because it is the employer's state of mind that is relevant, she must only show that the employer acted with malice or with reckless indifference to the lawfulness of his action. The Court also holds that an employer will not be vicariously liable for the discriminatory decisions of its managerial agents in cases where the decisions are contrary to the employer's good faith efforts to comply with Title VII. The Women's Rights Project joins in an amicus brief.

2000

United States v. Morrison, 529 U.S. 598 (2000). In this case brought under the civil rights remedy provision of the Violence Against Women Act (VAWA), which permits victims of gender-motivated violence to sue their attackers under federal law, the Supreme Court holds that: (1) the Commerce Clause does not provide Congress with authority to enact the civil rights remedy provision of VAWA, and (2) the enforcement clause of the Fourteenth Amendment does not provide Congress with the authority to enact the civil rights remedy.

Reeves v. Sanderson Plumbing Products, Inc., 530 U.S. 133 (2000). The Court holds that a jury may in some circumstances find gender discrimination in violation of Title VII based on evidence that the reasons an employer gives for an employment decision are untrue, even in the absence of any direct evidence of discrimination. The Women's Rights Project participates as amicus.

2001

Ferguson v. City of Charleston, 532 U.S. 67 (2001). In this case involving a South Carolina hospital that tests pregnant women for substance abuse and reports positive results to the police, the Court holds that pregnant women cannot be subject to warrantless, suspicionless searches simply because they are pregnant. The Women's Rights Project co-authors an amicus brief in this case.

Pollard v. E.I. Dupont Nemours Co., 532 U.S. 843 (2001). The Women's Rights Project joins an amicus brief in this case in which the Supreme Court holds that "front pay"— a form of prospective relief awarded by courts in employment discrimination cases under Title VII—is not a form of "compensatory damages" subject to dollar caps. The plaintiff, Sharon Pollard, one of only a few women working in the historically male manufacturing plant of E.I. DuPont de Nemours and Company in Tennessee, sued after she was subjected to sexual harassment for several years by co-workers and supervisors who repeatedly taunted her for doing "men's work" and for holding a supervisory position over certain men.

Nguyen v. INS, 533 U.S. 53 (2001). The Women's Rights Project co-counsels this case challenging one of the few remaining statutes explicitly discriminating on the basis of gender. The law at issue automatically deems out-of-wedlock children born overseas to be United States citizens when their mothers are citizens, but requires affirmative steps acknowledging paternity before the child is 18 to establish the child's citizenship if only the father is a citizen. Voting 5-4 the Court holds the law to be constitutional, over a strong dissent by Justice O'Connor.

2003

Nevada Department of Human Resources v. Hibbs, 2003 WL 21210426. The Supreme Court holds that it is constitutional for a state to be sued in federal court for money damages when that state has violated the Family Medical Leave Act (FMLA). The FMLA provides 12 weeks unpaid leave to employees to care for a new baby or seriously ill family member. The Supreme Court holds that the act's guarantee of leave to all workers, regardless of their gender, attacked the stereotype formally perpetuated by many state employers that care giving was a woman's responsibility rather than a man's. Such stereotypes stigmatized female employees, the Court holds, and discouraged men from taking on family responsibilities. The Court thus concludes that the FMLA's guarantee of leave protected against such discriminatory stereotypes. The Women's Rights Project joins in an amicus brief.

Permission for use of this timeline granted by the ACLU Women's Rights Project.

ENDNOTES

1   LEE EPSTEIN & JACK KNIGHT, THE CHOICES JUSTICES MAKE (1998).
2   Frontiero v. Richardson, 411 U.S. 677 (1973).
3   U.S. CONST. amend. XIV.
4   *Id.*
5   Ruth Bader Ginsburg, Speech at the Minnesota ACLU (June 1977) (on file with the Library of Congress, Ginsburg Collection, Accession 2, Speeches and Writings File, Box 35 at 12) [hereinafter Minnesota ACLU Speech].
6   BARBARA A. PERRY, THE SUPREMES 115 (David A. Shultz ed., 1999).
7   *Id.* at 115-26.
8   LINDA KERBER, NO CONSTITUTIONAL RIGHT TO BE LADIES: WOMEN AND THE OBLIGATIONS OF CITIZENSHIP 202 (1998).
9   Malvina Halberstam, *Ruth Bader Ginsburg: The First Jewish Woman on the United States Supreme Court*, 19 CARDOZO L. REV. 1441, 1442 (1998).
10   *Id.* at 1443.
11   *Id.*
12   *Id.*
13   *Id.* at 1446.
14   *Id.*
15   Halberstam, *supra* note 9, at 1447.
16   *See id.*
17   *Id.* at 1448.
18   As of the time the article was written in 2001.

19   U.S. v. Virginia, 518 U.S. 515 (1996).

20   *Id.* at 524.

21   *See id.* at 566 (Scalia, J., dissenting).

22   Henry J. Abraham and Barbara A. Perry, Freedom and the Court: Civil Rights and Liberties in the United States 412 (7th ed. 1998).

23   Nadine Strossen, *The American Civil Liberties Union and Women's Rights,* 66 N.Y.U. L. Rev. 1940, 1941 (1991).

24   *Id.*

25   *Id.* at 1942-43.

26   *Id.*

27   *Id.* at 1943. *See also id.* at nn.14-15.

28   *Id.* at 1946-47.

29   Strossen, *supra* note 24, at 1947.

30   *Id.* at 1947-48.

31   Betty Friedan, The Feminine Mystique (1963).

32   David & Myra Sadker, Failing At Fairness: How America's Schools Cheat Girls (1994).

33   Strossen, *supra* note 23, at 1948-49.

34   Kerber, *supra* note 8, at 202.

35   Strossen, *supra* note 23, at 1949 n.54.

36   *Id.* at 1949. *See also* White v. Crook, 251 F. Supp. 401 (M.D. Ala. 1966).

37   368 U.S. 57 (1961).

38   *See White,* 251 F. Supp. 401.

39   404 U.S. 71 (1971).

40   Halberstam, *supra* note 9, at 1447.

41   Ginsburg Collection, Accession 1, Speeches and Writings File, Box 16.

42   Ginsburg was a part-time staff attorney, dividing her time between the WRP and her duties as Professor of Law at Columbia University. Brenda Feigen Fasteau was the full-time staff attorney at the WRP.

43   Strossen, *supra* note 23, at 1950. "[T]he ACLU's work on civil liberties and civil rights parallels the perceived [difference] between these two sets of issues, which ... stem[s] from the

[government's role] with respect to each. Civil liberties involve limits on the government's power ... [whereas] the protection of civil rights [necessitates] government action to ensure that all people are treated equally and to [provide remedies for] past discrimination." *Id.* at 1941-42.

[44] *Id.* at 1950. *See also* 2 ACLU Women's Rights Report 5 (1980).

[45] ACLU Women's Rights Project prospectus [hereinafter Prospectus], Ginsburg Collection, Accession 1, ACLU File, Box 11 at 2.

[46] Ginsburg cites the Equal Pay Act of 1963, Title VII of the Civil Rights Act of 1964, and Title IX of the Education Amendments of 1972. Shortly after the WRP was founded, Congress amended Title VI to include sex discrimination as a trigger for the denial of federal funds to public or private programs and activities. ABRAHAM & PERRY, *supra* note 22, at 413.

[47] Prospectus, *supra* note 45, at 1.

[48] 20 U.S.C. §§ 1681-1688 (1994).

[49] SADKER, *supra* note 32, at 36.

[50] The six core areas, in detail, included: (1) Employment—workmen's compensation, leaves of absence for child bearing, and disability insurance for pregnancy; (2) Private Institutions—governmental aid and benefits to institutions that exclude, segregate, or discriminate on the basis of sex; (3) Reproductive control—the right to abortion, right to be voluntarily sterilized, and right not to be involuntarily sterilized; (4) Education—sex discrimination in admissions to schools or programs; (5) Training programs—effective enforcement of anti-discrimination laws in government training programs; (6) Credit—discrimination by sex in availability of loans, mortgages, credit cards, and home rentals. *See* Prospectus, *supra* note 49, at 4.

[51] *Id.* at 5.

[52] Ruth Bader Ginsburg, Women as Full Members of the Club: An Evolving American Ideal (Mar. 12, 1976) (on file with the Library of Congress, Ginsburg Collection, Accession 2, Speeches and Writings File, Box 35, at 2).

[53] 83 U.S. 130, 140 (1872).

[54]   83 U.S. 36 (1872).

[55]   *See id.*

[56]   Ruth Bader Ginsburg, Toward Elimination of Sex Based Discrimination: Constitutional Aspects, (Aug. 1, 1972) (unpublished draft, on file with the Library of Congress, Ginsburg Collection, Accession 2, Speeches and Writings File, Box 34 at 3) [hereinafter Toward Elimination].

[57]   208 U.S. 412, 423 (1908).

[58]   Ginsburg, *supra* note 52, at 4. *See also* Lochner v. New York, 198 U.S. 45 (1905).

[59]   335 U.S. 464, 466 (1948).

[60]   368 U.S. 57 (1961).

[61]   *Id.* at 62.

[62]   *See* Strossen, *supra* note 23, at 1950.

[63]   *See generally* KERBER, *supra* note 8.

[64]   *See id.* at 201.

[65]   Brief for the ACLU, Reed v. Reed, 404 U.S. 71 (1971) (No. 430).

[66]   KERBER, *supra* note 8, at 199.

[67]   Pauli Murray & Mary Eastwood, *Jane Crow and the Law: Sex Discrimination and Title VII*, 34 GEO. WASH. L. REV. 232 (1965). Ginsburg was also greatly influenced by LEO KANOWITZ, WOMEN AND THE LAW (1969).

[68]   KERBER, *supra* note 8, at 202.

[69]   404 U.S. 71 (1971).

[70]   Ginsburg's internal memorandum on Reed, June 2001 draft (on file with the Library of Congress, Ginsburg Collection, Accession 1, ACLU file, Box 6).

[71]   Ruth Bader Ginsburg, *Constitutional Adjudication in the United States As A Means Of Advancing the Equal Stature of Men and Women Under the Law*, 26 HOFSTRA L. REV. 263, 267 (1997). *See also Reed*, 404 U.S. 71.

[72]   *See Reed*, 404 U.S. at 73. IDAHO CODE § 15-312 (Michie 1970) provided: "Administration of the estate of a person dying intestate must be granted to some one or more of the persons hereinafter mentioned, and they are respectively entitled thereto

in the following order: 1. The surviving husband or wife or some competent person whom he or she may request to have appointed. 2. The children. 3. The father or mother. 4. The brothers. 5. The sisters. 6. The grandchildren. 7. The next of kin entitled to share in the distribution of the estate. 8. Any of the kindred. 9. The public administrator. 10. The creditors of such person at the time of death. 11. Any person legally competent. If the decedent was a member of a partnership at the time of his decease, the surviving partner must in no case be appointed administrator of his estate." Section 15-314 provided: "of several persons claiming and equally entitled ... to administer, males must be preferred to females, and relatives of the whole to those of the half blood." 404 U.S. at 73.

[73]   Ginsburg, *supra* note 52, at 267.

[74]   Appellee's Brief, Reed v. Reed, 404 U.S. 71 (1971) (No. 430) (on file with the Library of Congress, Ginsburg Collection, Accession 1, ACLU File, Box 6, at 5) [hereinafter *Reed* Appellee's Brief].

[75]   *Id.* at 7.

[76]   *Id.* at 8.

[77]   253 U.S. 412 (1920).

[78]   Appellant's Brief, Reed v. Reed, 404 U.S. 71(1971) (No. 430) (on file with the Library of Congress, Ginsburg Collection, Accession 1, ACLU File, Box 6, at 8) [hereinafter *Reed* Appellant's Brief].

[79]   *Id.* at 9.

[80]   *Id.* at 8.

[81]   *See* Reed, 404 U.S. 71.

[82]   *Reed Appellant's* Brief, *supra* note 78, at 60.

[83]   *See* F.S. Royster Guano Co. v. Virginia, 253 U.S. 412 (1920).

[84]   *Reed Appellant's* Brief, *supra* note 78, at 60.

[85]   *Id.* at 62.

[86]   *Id.*

[87]   *Reed* Appellee's Brief, *supra* note 74, at 13.

[88]   *Id.* at 6.

[89]   *Id.* at 13.

[90] *See* Reed, 404 U.S. 71.

[91] *See* Muller v. Oregon, 208 U.S. 412 (1908).

[92] *Reed* Appellant's Brief, *supra* note 78, at 66.

[93] Ruth Bader Ginsburg & Barbara Flagg, *Some Reflections on the Feminist Legal Thought of the 1970s*, 1 U. CHI. LEGAL F. 9, 18 (1989).

[94] *See Reed*, 404 U.S. 71.

[95] GUNNAR MYRDAL ET AL., AN AMERICAN DILEMMA: THE NEGRO PROBLEM AND MODERN DEMOCRACY (1944).

[96] SIMONE DE BEAUVOIR, THE SECOND SEX (H.M. Parshley ed. & trans., Vintage Books 1989) (1949).

[97] *See Reed* Appellant's Brief, *supra* note 78, section IB, at 14-41.

[98] HENRIK IBSEN, A DOLL'S HOUSE (James McFarlane trans., Oxford University Press 1961) (1879).

[99] ALEXIS DE TOCQUEVILLE, DEMOCRACY IN AMERICA (George Lawrence trans. & J.P. Mayer ed., 1969).

[100] *Reed* Appellant's Brief, *supra* note 78, at 13.

[101] *Id.*

[102] 163 U.S. 537 (1896).

[103] *Reed* Appellant's Brief, *supra* note 78, at 15.

[104] *Id.*, at 18.

[105] *Id.* at 29. *See also* MYRDAL, *supra* note 95.

[106] Of the four decisions, Ginsburg addressed *Muller*, *Goesaert*, and *Hoyt*. *Bradwell* was followed in re Lockwood, 154 U.S. 116 (1984). Both decisions were overruled sub silentio by *Konigsberg v. State Bar of California*, 353 U.S. 252, 262 (1957) and *Schware v. Board of Bar Examiners*, 353 U.S. 232, 239-49 (1957).

[107] *See* 208 U.S. 412 (1908).

[108] *Reed* Appellant's Brief, *supra* note 89, at 43, 45. The Ninth Circuit, in *Mengelkoch v. Indus. Welfare Comm'n*, 437 F. 2d 563 (1971), held, among other things, that *Muller* had long ago lost its vitality because federal courts no longer made the kind of due process inquiry present there.

[109] 335 U.S. 464 (1948).

[110] 368 U.S. 57 (1961).

[111] *Goesaert*, 335 U.S. at 466.

112 347 U.S. 483 (1954).

113 364 U.S. 51 (1960).

114 Lower courts had made clear that Goesaert was no longer, if ever, considered vital. See Paterson Tavern & Grill Owner's Ass'n v. Hawthorne, 270 A. 2d 628, 630-31 (N.J. 1970); Seidenberg v. McSorely's Old Ale House, 317 F. Supp. 593 (S.D.N.Y. 1970). In addition, Ginsburg was most impressed by Sail'er Inn, Inc. v. Kirby, 485 P. 2d 529 (Cal. 1971), which was the first decision to declare unequivocally that sex is a suspect classification.

115 239 U.S. 33 (1915).

116 Id. at 41.

117 See Toward Elimination, supra note 56.

118 Goesaert v. Cleary, 335 U.S. 464, 466 (1948).

119 334 U.S. 410 (1948).

120 Toward Elimination, supra note 56, at 5.

121 Id.

122 See White v. Crook, 251 F. Supp. 401 (M.D. Ala. 1966).

123 313 N.Y.S.2d 827, 830 (Sup. Ct. 1970).

124 405 U.S. 625 (1972).

125 Alexander, 405 U.S. at 633.

126 Peters v. Kiff, 407 U.S. 493 (1972).

127 421 U.S. 772 (1975).

128 Reed Appellant's Brief, supra note 78, at 51.

129 See Reed, 404 U.S. 71.

130 Reed Appellant's Brief, supra note 78, at 55.

131 Id.

132 Struck v. Sec'y of Def., 409 U.S. 947 (1972).

133 Frontiero v. Richardson, 411 U.S. 677 (1973).

134 Ginsburg's internal memorandum on Reed, supra note 70.

135 Id.

136 Reed, 404 U.S. 71.

137 See High Court Outlaws Sex Discrimination, NEW YORK POST, Vol. 171 No. 6. (1971).

138 See Frontiero, 411 U.S. 677.

139 Ginsburg's internal memorandum on Reed, supra note 70.

140   *Id.* at 10.
141   *Reed,* 404 U.S. 71.
142   ABRAHAM & PERRY, *supra* note 22, at 414. For an excellent commentary on gender discrimination cases, see Chapter 8, "Gender and Race Under the New Equal Protection."
143   *See Reed,* 404 U.S. 71.
144   429 U.S. 190 (1976).
145   405 U.S. 438 (1972).
146   *Id.* at 447 n.7. *See also* Griswold v. Connecticut, 381 U.S. 479 (1965).
147   *See* 469 F.2d 466 (10th Cir. 1972); Letter from Ruth Bader Ginsburg to Gerald Gunther (December 26, 1972) (on file with the Library of Congress, Ginsburg Collection, Accession 2, ACLU file, Box 30).
148   *See* 411 U.S. 677 (1973); Letter from Ruth Bader Ginsburg to Gerald Gunther (December 26, 1972) (on file with the Library of Congress, Ginsburg Collection, Accession 2, ACLU file, Box 30).
149   Gerald Gunther, *Foreword: In Search of Evolving Doctrine on a Changing Court: A Model for a Newer Equal Protection,* 86 HARV. L. REV. 1 (1972).
150   *See id.*
151   *See Reed,* 404 U.S. 71.
152   Gunther, *supra* note 149, at 20.
153   *Id.* at 19-20.
154   *Id.* at 21.
155   408 U.S. 92 (1972) (involving an ordinance that exempted peaceful labor picketing from its ban on picketing near school buildings).
156   *Id.* at 95.
157   Gunther, *supra* note 149, at 17.
158   404 U.S. 71 (1971).
159   469 F.2d 466 (10th Cir. 1972).
160   Ruth Bader Ginsburg, Keynote Address at Hawaii ACLU Conference on Women's Legal Rights (Mar. 16-17, 1978) (on file with the Library of Congress, Ginsburg Collection, Accession

1, Speeches and Writings File, Box 15, at 8) [hereinafter ACLU address].

[161] *Id.*

[162] *Id.*

[163] *High Court Outlaws Sex Discrimination*, NEW YORK POST, Vol. 171 No. 6 (1971).

[164] ACLU address, *supra* note 160, at 9.

[165] 420 U.S. 636 (1975).

[166] 430 U.S. 199 (1976).

[167] 411 U.S. 677 (1973).

[168] Frontiero v. Laird, 341 F. Supp. 201, 203 (M.D. Ala. 1972).

[169] *Id.* at 209.

[170] *See Frontiero*, 411 U.S. 677.

[171] Letter from Ruth Bader Ginsburg to Charles Abernathy and Joe Levin (Oct. 16, 1972) (on file with the Library of Congress, Ginsburg Collection, Accession 1, ACLU file, Box 3).

[172] For complete detail of the arguments in the correspondence between Ginsburg and Levin, see generally the series of letters in October 1972 (on file with the Library of Congress, Ginsburg Collection, Accession 1, ACLU File, Box 3.)

[173] Id.

[174] Letter from Charles Abernathy to Brenda Fasteau (Oct. 19, 1972) (on file with the Library of Congress, Ginsburg Collection, Accession 1, ACLU file, Box 3).

[175] *Id.*

[176] Letter from Joseph Levin to Melvin Wulf (Oct. 17, 1972) (on file with the Library of Congress, Ginsburg Collection, Accession 1, ACLU File, Box 3).

[177] Letter from Ruth Bader Ginsburg to Joseph Levin (Oct. 24, 1972) (on file with the Library of Congress, Ginsburg Collection, Accession 1, ACLU File, Box 3).

[178] Letter from Joseph Levin to Ruth Bader Ginsburg (Oct. 27, 1972) (on file with the Library of Congress, Ginsburg Collection, Accession 1, ACLU File, Box 3).

[179] *Id.*

[180] Letter from Ruth Bader Ginsburg to Joseph Levin (Oct. 31,

1972) (on file with the Library of Congress, Ginsburg Collection, Accession 1, ACLU File, Box 3).

181   409 U.S. 947 (1972).
182   Ruth Bader Ginsburg, *Speaking In a Judicial Voice*, 67 N.Y.U.L. REV. 1185, 1200 (1992).
183   Reed Appellant's Brief, supra note 78.
184   Ginsburg, *supra* note 182, at 1201.
185   409 U.S. 1107 (1973).
186   *Toward Elimination, supra* note 56, at 16.
187   398 U.S. 333, 361-67 (1970) (Harlan, J., concurring).
188   *Toward Elimination, supra* note 56, at 16.
189   Letter from Ruth Bader Ginsburg to Gerald Gunther, December 26, 1972 (on file with the Library of Congress, Ginsburg Collection, Accession 1, ACLU file, Box 3).
190   Appellant's Brief, Frontiero v. Richardson, 411 U.S. 677 (1973) (No. 71-1694) (on file with the Library of Congress, Ginsburg Collection, Accession 1, ACLU File, Box 3, at 38) [hereinafter *Frontiero* Appellant's Brief].
191   *Id.* at 41.
192   *Frontiero* Appellant's Brief, *supra* note 190, at 8.
193   *Id.* at 47.
194   *Id.* at 51.
195   Amicus Brief of the ACLU, *Frontiero v. Richardson, 411 U.S. 677 (1973)* (on file with the Library of Congress, Ginsburg Collection, Accession 1, ACLU File, Box 3, at 46) [hereinafter *Frontiero* Amicus].
196   405 U.S. 645 (1972).
197   *Frontiero* Amicus, *supra* note 195, at 50.
198   464 F.2d 533 (9th Cir. 1972).
199   *Frontiero* Amicus, *supra* note 195, at 50.
200   *Id.*
201   341 F. Supp. 217 (M.D. Ala. 1971), *aff'd mem.*, 405 U.S. 970 (1972).
202   *Frontiero* Amicus, *supra* note 195, at 49.
203   *Id.*
204   405 U.S. 438 (1972).

[205] Letter from Joseph Levin to Ruth Bader Ginsburg (Oct. 27, 1972), *supra* note 178.

[206] *See* Muller v. Oregon, 208 U.S. 412 (1908).

[207] *See* Goesaert v. Cleary, 335 U.S. 464 (1948).

[208] *See* Hoyt v. Florida, 368 U.S. 57 (1961).

[209] *Frontiero* Appellant's Brief, *supra* note 190, at 29.

[210] *Id.* at 32.

[211] *Id.* at 36.

[212] *Frontiero* Appellant's Brief, *supra* note 190, at 57.

[213] *Frontiero* Amicus, *supra* note 195, at 19.

[214] *See Reed*, 404 U.S. 71.

[215] *Frontiero* Amicus, *supra* note 195, at 23.

[216] *Id.* at 7.

[217] *Id.* at 8.

[218] *Id.* at 27.

[219] 83 U.S. 36 (1872).

[220] *Frontiero* Amicus, *supra* note 195, at 28.

[221] *Id.* at 34.

[222] 456 F.2d 18 (10th Cir. 1972).

[223] 340 F. Supp. 886 (D.S.C. 1972).

[224] *Frontiero* Amicus, *supra* note 234, at 33. For a complete listing of both categories, see *id.* at 32-33.

[225] 83 U.S. 130 (1872).

[226] 88 U.S. 162 (1874).

[227] *Frontiero* Amicus, *supra* note 195, at 36.

[228] PAULI MURRAY, THE RIGHTS OF WOMEN, THE RIGHTS OF AMERICANS: WHAT THEY ARE, WHAT THEY SHOULD BE (1971).

[229] *Frontiero* Amicus, *supra* note 195, at 39.

[230] 239 U.S. 33 (1915).

[231] *Frontiero* Amicus, *supra* note 195, at 39.

[232] 405 U.S. 625 (1972).

[233] 407 U.S. 493 (1972).

[234] *Frontiero* Amicus, *supra* note 195, at 42.

[235] 405 U.S. 134 (1972).

[236] *See Reed*, 404 U.S. 71.

[237] Appellees' Brief, *Frontiero v. Richardson, 411 U.S. 677 (1973)*

(on file with the Library of Congress, Ginsburg Collection, ACLU File, Box 3, at 12) [hereinafter *Frontiero* Appellees' Brief].

[238] Id at 13. *See also* Shapiro v. Thompson, 394 U.S. 618 (1969).

[239] *Frontiero* Appellees' Brief, *supra* note 237, at 15.

[240] Appellants' Reply Brief, *Frontiero v. Richardson, 411 U.S. 677 (1973) (on file with the Library of Congress,* Ginsburg Collection, Accession 1, ACLU File, Box 3, at 7) [hereinafter *Frontiero* Reply].

[241] *Frontiero* Appellees' Brief, *supra* note 237, at 16.

[242] *Frontiero* Reply, *supra* note 240, at 9.

[243] Id.

[244] *Frontiero* Appellees' Brief, *supra* note 237, at 9.

[245] Id. at 10.

[246] Brown v. Bd. of Educ., 347 U.S. 483 (1952).

[247] *Frontiero* Reply, *supra* note 240, at 11.

[248] Id. at 13.

[249] 411 U.S. at 691 (1973) (Rehnquist, J., dissenting).

[250] Bob Woodward & Scott Armstrong, The Brethren: Inside the Supreme Court (1979).

[251] Woodward & Armstrong, *supra* note 250, at 300. For a detailed account of the inner working of the Court, see *id.* at 300-03.

[252] Id. at 302.

[253] *See generally* Woodward & Armstrong, *supra* note 250.

[254] Comment of Ruth Bader Ginsburg on *Frontiero v. Richardson* for *Women's Rights Law Reporter* (on file with the Library of Congress, Ginsburg Collection, Accession 1, ACLU File, Box 3, at 4) [hereinafter *Frontiero* Comment].

[255] *Frontiero*, 411 U.S. at 688.

[256] Id. at 691.

[257] *Frontiero* Comment, *supra* note 254, at 6.

[258] Amy Walsh, *Ruth Bader Ginsburg: Extending the Constitution*, 32 J. Marshall L. Rev. 197, 202 (1998).

[259] ACLU Address, *supra* note 160, at 17.

[260] *Frontiero* Comment, *supra* note 254, at 5.

[261] Id. at 7.

[262] Id.

263   *Id.* at 8.
264   410 U.S. 113 (1973).
265   Ginsburg, *supra* note 182, at 1202. *See also Struck*, 409 U.S. 947; *Roe v. Wade*, 410 U.S. 113 (1973).
266   *See Struck*, 409 U.S. 947.
267   Ginsburg, *supra* note 182, at 1201.
268   ACLU Address, *supra* note 160, at 12.
269   *Id* at 13.
270   420 U.S. 636 (1975).
271   430 U.S. 924 (1977).
272   ACLU Address, *supra* note 160, at 14.
273   Ruth Bader Ginsburg to Jack Blumenfeld, October 24, 1974, Ginsburg Collection, Accession 1, ACLU File, Box 4.
274   ACLU Address, *supra* note 160, at 15.
275   *See Kahn*, 416 U.S. 351.
276   *See id.*
277   Letter from Ruth Bader Ginsburg to Mary McGowan Davis, January 30, 1974 (on file with the Library of Congress, Ginsburg Collection, Accession 1, ACLU File, Box 4).
278   Appellants' Brief, *Kahn v. Shevin*, 349 U.S. 351 (1974) (on file with the Library of Congress, Ginsburg Collection, Accession 1, ACLU File, Box 4, at 24) [hereinafter *Kahn* Brief].
279   404 U.S. 71 (1971).
280   411 U.S. 677 (1973).
281   *Kahn* Brief, *supra* note 278, at 4.
282   368 U.S. 57 (1961).
283   *Kahn* Brief, *supra* note 278, at 6.
284   *Id.* at 5.
285   *Id.* at 6.
286   *Id.* at 7.
287   *Id.* at 6.
288   *Id.* at 5.
289   1891 Fla. Laws Ch. 4010. *See also* FLA. CONST., art. IX, §9 (1885).
290   *Kahn* Brief, *supra* note 356, at 8. For a complete history of the evolution of the statute, see *id.* at 8 n.4.

291 *Id.* at 8.
292 Mortiz v. Comm'r, 469 F.2d 466 (10th Cir. 1972) *cert denied*, 411 U.S. 677 (1973).
293 *Reed*, 404 U.S. at 75.
294 *Kahn* Brief, *supra* note 278, at 10.
295 *Id.*
296 *Id.*
297 *Kahn* Brief, *supra* note 278, at 12.
298 404 U.S. 645 (1972).
299 485 P.2d 529 (Cal. 1971).
300 *See id.*
301 Moritz v. Comm'r, supra note 292.
302 81 Cal. Rptr. 910 (Cal. Ct. App. 1969).
303 *Id.* at 913.
304 *Kahn* Brief, *supra* note 278, at 15.
305 390 F.2d 591 (2nd Cir.), *cert. denied*, 393 U.S. 982 (1968).
306 Frontiero Amicus, supra note 195.
307 42 U.S. 772 (1975).
308 *Kahn* Brief, *supra* note 278, at 17.
309 313 N.Y.S.2d 827 (Sup. Ct. 1970).
310 *Kahn* Brief, *supra* note 278, at 16.
311 Goesaert v. Cleary, 335 U.S. 464, 466 (1948). See also Kahn Brief, *supra* note 278, at 23.
312 473 F.2d 629 (2d Cir. 1973).
313 *Kahn* Brief, *supra* note 278, at 24.
314 *Id.*
315 420 U.S. 636 (1975).
316 *Kahn* Brief, *supra* note 278, at18.
317 *Id.*
318 F.S. Royster Guano Co. v. Virginia, 253 U.S. 412, 415 (1920).
319 *F.S. Royster Guano*, 253 U.S. at 415. *See also Appellees' Brief*, Kahn v. Shevin, 416 U.S. 351 (1974) (No. 73-78) (on file with the Library of Congress, Ginsburg Collection, Accession 1, ACLU File, Box 4, at 15) [hereinafter *Kahn* Appellees' Brief].
320 *Kahn* Appellees' Brief, *supra* note 319, at 15.
321 *Id.* at 10.

322 *Moritz*, 469 F.2d at 470.
323 *Frontiero*, 411 U.S. at 690-91.
324 *Kahn* Appellees' Brief, *supra* note 278, at 24.
325 *Id.* at 22.
326 *Id.* at 26.
327 *Id.* at 27.
328 Notes of Justice William O. Douglas regarding *Kahn v. Shevin*, 416 U.S. 351 (1974), (Jan. 1, 1974) (on file with the Library of Congress, William O. Douglas Collection, Box 652) [hereinafter Douglas' *Kahn* notes].
329 *Id.*
330 *Id.*
331 *Kahn*, 416 U.S. at 360-62 (White, J., dissenting).
332 *Id.* at 357-60 (Brennan, J., dissenting).
333 Douglas' *Kahn* notes, *supra* note 328.
334 *Kahn*, 416 U.S. at 352-56.
335 Letter from Ruth Bader Ginsburg to Sara-Ann Determan (Apr. 26, 1974) (on file with the Library of Congress, Ginsburg Collection, Accession 1, ACLU File, Box 4).
336 416 U.S. 312 (1974).
337 ACLU address, *supra* note 160, at 10.
338 *Id.*
339 Letter from Ruth Bader Ginsburg to Bill Hoppe (Mar. 8, 1974) (on file with the Library of Congress, Ginsburg Collection, Accession 1, ACLU File, Box 4).
340 *DeFunis*, 416 U.S. at 319-20.
341 *Id.* at 320-48 (Douglas, J., dissenting).
342 Letter from Ruth Bader Ginsburg to Norman Dorsen (Apr. 30, 1974) (on file with the Library of Congress, Ginsburg Collection, Accession 1, ACLU File, Box 4).
343 Letter from Ruth Bader Ginsburg to E.S. Read (May 2, 1975), (on file with the Library of Congress, Ginsburg Collection, Accession 1, ACLU File, Box 4).
344 ACLU address, *supra* note 160, at 10.
345 William O. Douglas, Go East, Young Man (1974).
346 Letter from Ruth Bader Ginsburg to Bill Hoppe (June 16, 1975)

(on file with the Library of Congress, Ginsburg Collection, Accession 1, ACLU File, Box 4).

[347] *See* Weinberger v. Wiesenfeld, 420 U.S. 636 (1975).

[348] Letter from Ruth Bader Ginsburg to E.S. Read (Sept. 16, 1974) (on file with the Library of Congress, Ginsburg Collection, Accession 1, ACLU File, Box 4).

[349] 419 U.S. 498 (1975).

[350] Ruth Bader Ginsburg, Speech at the Minnesota ACLU (June 1977) (on file with the Library of Congress, Ginsburg Collection, Accession 2, Speeches and Writings File, Box 35 at 9) [hereinafter Minnesota ACLU speech].

[351] *Id.* at 10.

[352] *Schlesinger*, 409 U.S. at 510.

[353] *See id.*

[354] *Schlesinger*, 409 U.S. at 511 (Brennan, J., dissenting).

[355] Letter from Ruth Bader Ginsburg to Jack Blumenfeld (Oct. 24, 1974) (on file with the Library of Congress, Ginsburg Collection, Accession 1, ACLU File, Box 4).

[356] 416 U.S. 351 (1974).

[357] *Kahn*, 416 U.S. 351.

[358] 414 U.S. 632 (1974).

[359] 409 U.S. 947 (1972).

[360] *See LaFleur*, 414 U.S. 632.

[361] Amicus Brief of the ACLU, Cohen v. Chesterfield County School Board, (No. 72-1129) (adapted from Phillips v. Martin Marietta Corp., 416 F. 2d 1257, 1258 (5th Cir. 1969) (Brown, C.J., dissenting)) (on file with the Library of Congress, United States Supreme Court Records and Briefs, Vol. 414 at 9) [hereinafter *Cohen* Amicus].

[362] LaFleur, 465 F.2d at 1188 (6th Cir. 1972).

[363] *Cohen* Amicus, *supra* note 361, at 8.

[364] Reed v. Reed, 404 U.S. 71 (1971).

[365] Frontiero v. Richardson, 411 U.S. 677 (1973).

[366] 410 U.S. 113 (1973).

[367] 410 U.S. 959 (1973).

[368] *Cohen* Amicus, *supra* note 361, at 28.

[369] *See* Schattman v. Tex. Employment Comm'n, 459 F.2d 32 (5th Cir. 1972), *cert. denied*, 409 U.S. 1107 (1973).

[370] Letter from Ruth Bader Ginsburg to Mary Ellen Schattman (Feb. 18, 1973) (on file with the Library of Congress, Ginsburg Collection, Accession 1, ACLU File, Box 7).

[371] *See Schattman*, 409 U.S. 1107.

[372] 476 F.2d 92 (10th Cir. 1973).

[373] *Id.* at 96.

[374] *Cohen* Amicus, *supra* note 361, at 29.

[375] *See* LaFleur v. Cleveland Bd. of Educ., 414 U.S. 632 (1974).

[376] *Id.*

[377] *Id.* at 644.

[378] Amicus Brief of the ACLU, Geduldig v. Aiello, 417 U.S. 484 (1974) (No. 73-640) (on file with the Library of Congress, United States Supreme Court Records and Briefs, Vol. 417 at 7) [hereinafter *Aiello* Amicus].

[379] *See* Geduldig v. Aiello, 417 U.S. 484 (1974).

[380] Rentzer v. Cal. Unemployment Ins. App. Bd., 108 Cal. Rptr. 336 (Cal. Ct. App. 1973).

[381] 417 U.S. 484 (1974).

[382] Appellees' Brief, *Geduldig v. Aiello*, 417 U.S. 484 (1974) (No. 73-640) (on file with the Library of Congress, Ginsburg Collection, Accession 1, ACLU File, Box 7).

[383] *See Geduldig*, 417 U.S. 484.

[384] *Geduldig*, 417 U.S. at 503 (Brennan, J., dissenting).

[385] Minnesota ACLU Speech, *supra* note 350, at 11.

[386] *See* Turner v. Dep't of Employment Sec. of Utah, 423 U.S. 44 (1975).

[387] *See id.*

[388] Letter from Ruth Bader Ginsburg to Kathleen Peratis (Mar. 6, 1975) (on file with the Library of Congress, Ginsburg Collection, Accession 1, ACLU File, Box 9).

[389] Id.

[390] *See* 423 U.S. 44 (1975).

[391] *Id.*

[392] 429 U.S. 125 (1976).

393   434 U.S. 136 (1977).
394   Minnesota ACLU speech, *supra* note 350.
395   *Id.* at 137.
396   *Id.* at 140-41.
397   *Id.* at 144.
398   ACLU address, *supra* note 160, at 24.
399   Ruth Bader Ginsburg, George Abel Dreyfous Lecture (1978) (on file with the Library of Congress, Ginsburg Collection, Accession 1, Speeches and Writings File, Box 13 at 19) [hereinafter George Abel Dreyfous Lecture].
400   Id.
401   *Nashville Gas v. Satty*, 434 U.S. at 153-54 (Stevens, J., concurring).
402   ACLU address, *supra* note 160, at 24.
403   368 U.S. 57 (1961).
404   Taylor v. Louisiana, 419 U.S. 522 (1975).
405   42 U.S. 772 (1975).
406   Appellees' Brief, *Edwards v. Healy*, 42 U.S. 772 (1975) (No. 73-759) (on file with the Library of Congress, Ginsburg Collection, Accession 1, ACLU File, Box 4, at 12) [hereinafter Healy Brief].
407   *See* Reed v. Reed, 404 U.S. 71 (1971).
408   *See* Frontiero v. Richardson, 411 U.S. 677 (1973).
409   Healy Brief, supra note 406 at 17.
410   329 U.S. 187 (1946).
411   *Id.* at 193-94.
412   Healy Brief, supra note 406 at 14.
413   419 U.S. 522 (1975).
414   329 U.S. 187 (1946).
415   *Taylor*, 419 U.S. at 542 (Rehnquist, J., dissenting).
416   *Id.* at 540.
417   *Healy v. Edwards*, No. 73-759, Second Supplemental Memorandum Brief of Appellants Suggesting Mootness.
418   *See* 439 U.S. 357 (1979).
419   Memorandum of Ruth Bader Ginsburg on *Duren v. Missouri*, 439 U.S. 357 (1979), (May 31, 1979) (on file with the Library

of Congress, Ginsburg Collection, Accession 1, ACLU File, Box 3, at 3).

[420] Letter from Ruth Bader Ginsburg to Drew Days, May 29, 1979 (on file with the Library of Congress, Ginsburg Collection, Accession 1, ACLU File, Box 3).

[421] Minnesota ACLU Speech, supra note 350.

[422] See Frontiero v. Richardson, 411 U.S. 677 (1973).

[423] George Abel Dreyfous Lecture, supra note 399 at 22.

[424] 420 U.S. 636 (1975).

[425] See Kahn v. Shevin, 416 U.S. 351 (1974).

[426] See Geduldig v. Aiello, 417 U.S. 484 (1974).

[427] See Schlesinger v. Ballard, 419 U.S. 498 (1975).

[428] Wiesenfeld v. Weinberger, United States District Court of New Jersey, Civil Action No. 268-73.

[429] Letter from Ruth Bader Ginsburg to Stephen Wiesenfeld (December 27, 1972) (on file with the Library of Congress, Ginsburg Collection, Accession 1, ACLU File, Box 10).

[430] See Weinberger vs. Wiesenfeld, 420 U.S. 636 (1975).

[431] See Frontiero v. Richardson, 411 U.S. 677 (1973).

[432] Letter from Ruth Bader Ginsburg to Jane Lifset (May 15, 1973) (on file with the Library of Congress, Ginsburg Collection, Accession 1, ACLU File, Box 10).

[433] Plaintiff's Supplemental Brief, Wiesenfeld v. Weinberger, United States District Court, New Jersey (on file with Library of Congress, Ginsburg Collection, Accession 1, ACLU File, Box 10 at 6).

[434] 347 U.S. 483 (1952).

[435] Frontiero, 411 U.S. at 686.

[436] See Weinberger v. Wiesenfeld, 420 U.S. 636 (1975).

[437] Defendant's first supplemental memorandum (hereinafter Wiesenfeld Supplemental Motion), Weinberger v. Wiesenfeld, Ginsburg copy of memorandum. (On file with Library of Congress, Ginsburg Collection, Accession 1, ACLU File, Box 10).

[438] Wiesenfeld Supplemental Motion, supra note 437.

439   390 F.2d 591 (2d Cir. 1968).

440   *Wiesenfeld* Supplemental Motion, *supra* note 437, at 13.

441   395 F.2d 920 (2d Cir. 1968).

442   *Id.* at 931-32.

443   *See* Weinberger v. Wiesenfeld, 420 U.S. 636.

444   Letter from Ruth Bader Ginsburg to Jane Lifset (December 19, 1973) (on file with the Library of Congress, Ginsburg Collection, Accession 1, ACLU File, Box 10).

445   New Jersey District Court opinion, Ginsburg Copy, Ginsburg Collection, Accession 1, ACLU File, Box 10, at 11).

446   *Id. See also Frontiero*, 411 U.S. 677.

447   *See Weinberger*, 420 U.S. 636.

448   Letter from Ruth Bader Ginsburg to Stephen Wiesenfeld (March 19, 1974) (on file with the Library of Congress, Ginsburg Collection, Accession 1, ACLU File, Box 10).

449   *See Weinberger*, 420 U.S. 636.

450   Letter from Ruth Bader Ginsburg to Elizabeth Schneider (January 2, 1975) (on file with the Library of Congress, Ginsburg Collection, Accession 1, ACLU File, Box 10).

451   Appellee's Motion to Affirm, *Weinberger v. Wiesenfeld*, 420 U.S. 636 (1975) (No. 73-1892) (on file with the Library of Congress, Ginsburg Collection, Accession 1, ACLU File, Box 10, at 8).

452   Appellants' Brief, *Weinberger v. Wiesenfeld*, 420 U.S. 636 (1975) (No. 73-1892) (on file with the Library of Congress, Ginsburg Collection, Accession 1, ACLU File, Box 10, at 18).

453   *See* Frontiero, 411 U.S. 677.

454   *See* United States v. Virginia, 518 U.S. 515 (1996).

455   400 F. Supp. 953 (D.D.C. 1975).

456   ACLU address, *supra* note 160, at 17.

457   430 U.S. 199 (1976).

458   ACLU address, *supra* note 160, at 20.

459   George Abel Dreyfous Lecture, *supra* note 399, at 32.

460   429 U.S. 190 (1976).

461   Letter from Ruth Bader Ginsburg to Jill Laurie Goodman (Mar.

1, 1977) (on file with the Library of Congress, Ginsburg Collection, Accession 1, ACLU File, Box 2).

462 *Goldfarb*, 430 U.S. at 207 (quoting *Schlesinger v. Ballard*, 419 U.S. 498, 508 (1975)).

463 *Id.* at 217 (Stevens, J., concurring).

464 *Id.* at 223. *See also* Ruth Bader Ginsburg, *The Supreme Court Clarifies the Distinction Between Invidious Discrimination and Genuine Compensation* (Mar. 20, 1977) (unpublished draft, on file with the Library of Congress, Ginsburg Collection, Accession 1, ACLU File, Box 2 at 3) [hereinafter 1977 Draft].

465 Letter from Ruth Bader Ginsburg to Lawrence Wallace (Mar. 16, 1977) (on file with the Library of Congress, Ginsburg Collection, Accession 1, ACLU File, Box 2).

466 430 U.S. 924 (1977).

467 430 U.S. 313 (1977).

468 *See Webster*, 430 U.S. 313.

469 *Id.*

470 Letter from Jerry Lynch to Ruth Bader Ginsburg (Mar. 23, 1977) (on file with the Library of Congress, Ginsburg Collection, Accession 1, ACLU File, Box 2). Indicative of Ginsburg's camaraderie with Brennan's clerks is the postscript to Lynch's letter. He wrote: "Dave Barrett tells me that you said you felt like kissing Justice Brennan when you heard about Goldfarb. If so, you should save at least a handshake for the draftsman." She signed her reply "With more appreciation than a handshake could convey."

471 Letter from Ruth Bader Ginsburg to Jerry Lynch (Mar. 28, 1977) (on file with the Library of Congress, Ginsburg Collection, Accession 1, ACLU File, Box 2).

472 1977 Draft, *supra* note 464, at 5.

473 1977 Draft, *supra* note 464.

474 90 F. Supp. 21 (D.Me. 1950).

475 1977 Draft, *supra* note 464.

476 *See* Stanton v. Stanton, 429 U.S. 501 (1977).

477 1977 Draft, *supra* note 464, at 4.

478 438 U.S. 265 (1978).

479 George Abel Dreyfous lecture, *supra* note 399.

480 *Bakke*, 438 U.S. at 360 (Brennan, J., concurring in part and dissenting in part) (alteration in original) (quoting *Kahn v. Shevin*, 416 U.S. 351, 357 (1974) (Brennan, J., dissenting)).

481 *Bakke*, 438 U.S. at 358 (Brennan, J., concurring in part and dissenting in part).

482 *Bakke*, 438 U.S. at 362 (quoting Gunther, *supra* note 149, at 8).

483 440 U.S. 268 (1979).

484 443 U.S. 76 (1979).

485 446 U.S. 142 (1980).

486 Letter from Ruth Bader Ginsburg to John W. Reid (July 31, 1979) (on file with the Library of Congress, Ginsburg Collection, Accession 1, ACLU File, Box 11).

487 Letter from Ruth Bader Ginsburg to Isabelle Katz Pizler (July 25, 1979) (on file with the Library of Congress, Ginsburg Collection, Accession 1, ACLU File, Box 11.)

488 *See Wengler*, 446 U.S. 142.

489 Letter from Ruth Bader Ginsburg to John W. Reid (Aug. 17, 1979) (on file with the Library of Congress, Ginsburg Collection, Accession 1, ACLU File, Box 11).

490 *Wengler*, 446 U.S. at 153 (Rehnquist, J., dissenting).

491 *Court Backs Right of Inmates to Sue*, N.Y. TIMES, Apr. 23, 1980, at A22.

492 *See Wengler*, 446 U.S. 142.

493 Letter from Ruth Bader Ginsburg to Monica Blong Wagner, (Apr. 30, 1980) (on file with the Library of Congress, Ginsburg Collection, Accession 1, ACLU File, Box 11).

494 429 U.S. 190 (1976).

495 *See* Geduldig v. Aiello, 417 U.S. 484 (1974).

496 *See* LaFleur v. Cleveland Bd. of Educ., 414 U.S. 632 (1974).

497 Notes of Ruth Bader Ginsburg (Mar. 12, 1976) (on file with the Library of Congress, Ginsburg Collection, Accession 2, Speeches and Writings File, Box 35) [hereinafter Ginsburg 1976 notes].

498 *See* DeFunis v. Odegaard, 416 U.S. 312 (1974).

499 419 U.S. 522 (1975).

[500] 42 U.S. 772 (1975).

[501] Notes of Ruth Bader Ginsburg from League of Women Voters panel discussion (1976) (on file with the Library of Congress, Ginsburg Collection, Accession 2, Speeches and Writings File, Box 30, at 3) [hereinafter LWV panel notes].

[502] Ginsburg 1976 notes, *supra* note 497.

[503] *Id.*

[504] LWV panel notes, *supra* note 501.

[505] Ginsburg 1976 notes, *supra* note 497.

[506] CHARLOTTE OBSERVER, Aug. 30, 1976, p. A1, Ginsburg copy of article (on file with the Library of Congress, Ginsburg Collection, Accession 2, Miscellaneous File).

[507] Beer that contained 3.2% alcohol, or 3.2 beer, was commonly referred to as "near beer."

[508] *See* Craig v. Boren, 429 U.S. 190.

[509] Letter from Ruth Bader Ginsburg to Fred Gilbert (Jan. 15, 1976) (on file with the Library of Congress, Ginsburg Collection, Accession 1, ACLU File, Box 2).

[510] Memorandum from Mel Wulf to ACLU General Counsel (Jan. 16, 1976) (on file with the Library of Congress, Ginsburg Collection, Accession 1, ACLU File, Box 2).

[511] Letter from Fred Gilbert to Ruth Bader Ginsburg (Jan. 21, 1976) (on file with the Library of Congress, Ginsburg Collection, Accession 1, ACLU File, Box 2).

[512] Letter from Ruth Bader Ginsburg to Fred Gilbert (Jan. 30, 1976) (on file with the Library of Congress, Ginsburg Collection, Accession 1, ACLU File, Box 2).

[513] Letter from Ruth Bader Ginsburg to Fred Gilbert (Jan. 26, 1976) (on file with the Library of Congress, Ginsburg Collection, Accession 1, ACLU File, Box 2).

[514] Letter from Ruth Bader Ginsburg to Fred Gilbert (Feb. 19, 1976) (on file with the Library of Congress, Ginsburg Collection, Accession 1, ACLU File, Box 2).

[515] Letter from Ruth Bader Ginsburg to Bob Rightson (Feb. 20, 1976) (on file with the Library of Congress, Ginsburg Collection, Accession 1, ACLU File, Box 2).

516   Letter from Fred Gilbert to Ruth Bader Ginsburg (Feb. 27, 1976) (on file with the Library of Congress, Ginsburg Collection, Accession 1, ACLU File, Box 2).

517   Letter from Ruth Bader Ginsburg to Marilyn Levy (Feb. 26, 1976) (on file with the Library of Congress, Ginsburg Collection, Accession 1, ACLU File, Box 2). To clarify, Ginsburg later remarked that it was an embarrassment that such a ridiculous law should occupy the highest court in the nation. *See* Ginsburg 1976 notes, *supra* note 497.

518   Letter from Ruth Bader Ginsburg to Fred Gilbert (May 11, 1976) (on file with the Library of Congress, Ginsburg Collection, Accession 1, ACLU File, Box 2).

519   *See* Moose Lodge v. Irvis, 407 U.S. 163 (1972).

520   Letter from Ruth Bader Ginsburg to Fred Gilbert, (May 27, 1976) (on file with the Library of Congress, Ginsburg Collection, Accession 1, ACLU File, Box 2).

521   Letter from Ruth Bader Ginsburg to Fred Gilbert, (Aug. 13, 1976) (on file with the Library of Congress, Ginsburg Collection, Accession 1, ACLU File, Box 2) (see the blind carbon copy to Jill Hoffman).

522   Oral Argument transcript for *Craig v. Boren*, 429 U.S. 190 (1976) (on file with the Library of Congress, Ginsburg Collection, Accession 1, ACLU File, Box 2).

523   *Id.*

524   *Id.*

525   *Goesaert v. Cleary*, 335 U.S. 464, 465 (1948).

526   *Craig*, 429 U.S. at 197.

527   Letter from Warren Burger to William Brennan, (Nov. 15, 1976) notes, William J. Brennan Collection, Library of Congress, Craig v. Boren file.

528   WASHINGTON POST editorial(Dec. 21, 1976), Ginsburg copy of editorial (on file with the Library of Congress, Ginsburg Collection, Accession 1, ACLU File, Box 2).

529   Ruth Bader Ginsburg memorandum, May 21, 1979 (on file with the Library of Congress, Ginsburg Collection, ACLU File, Box 30)

530   Lyle Dennison, speech, Ruth Bader Ginsburg's Long March to VMI (on file with the Library of Congress, Ginsburg Collection, Accession 1).

531   Comments to author, July 2001. *See* Tuan Anh Nguyen. v. INS, 533 U.S. 53 (2001).

532   *See id.*

533   Lyle Denniston, WASHINGTON STAR, October 6, 1976, Ginsburg's copy of article (on file with the Library of Congress, Ginsburg Collection, Accession 1, ACLU File, Box 2 at 24)

Made in the USA
Lexington, KY
07 December 2015